STEAM IN CAMERA 1898–1960
Second Series

STEAM IN CAMERA
1898–1960
Second Series

Patrick Russell

Photographs from the LCGB Ken Nunn Collection

LONDON

IAN ALLAN LTD

First published 1981

ISBN 0 7110 1068 4

Published by Ian Allan Ltd, Shepperton, Surrey;
and printed by Ian Allan Printing Ltd at their works
at Coombelands in Runnymede, England

*Frontispiece: LNER Class A4 4-6-2 No 2509 Silver Link
gathers speed past Low Fell, three miles out from Newcastle,
with the 550ton up 'Flying Scotsman'. The photograph is one of
very few undocumented in the collection. It is undoubtedly
No 2509, for it can be distinguished by the straight handrail
along the side of the boiler and the position of the three oil box
doors in the streamline casing reaching down to the running
plate. As the number between the front buffers was not added
until about June 1936, and the season appears to be early
autumn, the picture must have been taken in October 1935 when
the engine was only one month old. It would therefore be a
Saturday during those first two hectic weeks when* Silver Link
*was operating the new 'Silver Jubilee' Monday-Friday service
single-handed.*

Introduction

Some eight or nine years ago I had the pleasure of compiling an album of photographs from the Ken Nunn Collection of the Locomotive Club of Great Britain. Returning after this timely interval to take a fresh look at the riches contained therein, I have prepared a completely new selection which again spans a period of over 60 years. First let me trace once more the career of this notable enthusiast who was employed in the railway service all his working life.

Kenneth Adrian Clement Roper Nunn was born at Broadstairs on 3 September 1891. The family moved to Brentwood during his early childhood, where his father had been appointed Curate of the local parish. He was educated at St Johns School, Leatherhead, and joined the Great Eastern Railway in 1910 as a clerk in the accounts offices at Liverpool Street. He used to recall that humble errands at that time took him regularly into the sanctum of Lord Claud Hamilton himself.

On the outbreak of World War I he enlisted in the Essex Regiment, but he was subsequently transferred to the Middlesex Regiment, only to be invalided out after being badly gassed during the campaign in Flanders in the autumn of 1915. He was very ill for a long time, and indeed lost his voice for some years.

After the war the family went its separate ways and Ken moved to Grove Park in 1922. He had returned to the GER, and was later based at Kings Cross in the years after the Grouping. He met his future wife, Marjorie, in 1931 and they were married in July 1932, setting up home in Wembley where he lived for the rest of his life.

Latterly he worked in the Public Relations office at Marylebone under George Dow, and was clearly in his element there engaged upon the photographic archives. He retired in 1952, and assisted John Scholes during the establishment of the Clapham museum contributing valuable advice on the merit of various prospective acquisitions.

He died on 8 April 1965, at the age of 73.

Ken Nunn had become the first President of the LCGB shortly after its formation in 1949, and continued to hold this appointment until his death. The story goes that the first candidate for the presidency had been Sir Eustace Missenden, then Chairman of the newly Nationalised British Railways. Ken was well aware of this rather presumptuous idea, and when he was approached instead replied with characteristic modesty 'Oh heavens, what a come-down!'

He left what was probably one of the finest, most knowledgeable and well-documented collections of railway photographs ever compiled. With no instructions for its disposal, his widow was most anxious that so far as possible it should be retained intact. Many members of the LCGB were, of course, well aware from personal contact and friendship, not to mention the absorbing and fascinating talks he had given to Club gatherings over the previous 16 years, of its immense value to railway history and literature. From here it was but a short and natural step for the Management Committee to conclude an agreement with Marjorie Nunn for the purchase of the whole collection, and to the appointment of trustees and a committee to administer and develop it for the benefit of all members.

What is it then that makes the photographs so especially interesting, and stirs such enthusiasm amongst those who know them well. He was lucky enough to have been born at almost the ideal time, first to witness the railway age reaching its zenith in those halcyon pre-Grouping years before 1914, then to savour the coming of the streamlined era and the high speed trains of the 1930s, and finally to lament the subsequent contraction and decline of railways after World War II. Certainly there were more accomplished photographers among his contemporaries, but he had few equals in achieving such a comprehensive record of the railway scene, and of locomotives in particular.

There are nearly 12,000 plates and negatives in the collection spanning the period from 1898 to 1960. This may not seem so remarkable when compared with the extravagant use of the 35mm camera in recent years. However, it should be remembered that times were not so affluent then, few people had motor cars and photographic techniques have advanced a long way since Ken first started. Nevertheless, he did rather stubbornly persist with the same hefty old reflex camera all his life, and it got too heavy for him in the end.

Not all the photographs are his own work, for he added to his collection the plates of his elder brother, Cyril, who had given up his interest around 1930. After World War I Cyril had lived successively in the Newcastle, Glasgow and Leeds areas, and they seldom met save on special occasions such as the Railway Centenary at Darlington in 1925. He also acquired the photographs of his friend, Harold Hopwood, once a prolific contributor of articles to railway journals, who had worked for the Great Northern Railway and died in 1926.

Quite apart from his association with the LCGB, Ken Nunn was well known amongst railway enthusiasts and could count many famous names as personal friends. From very early days he was a ceaseless contributor of photographs, articles and information to the *Railway Magazine* and other publications. He had been a member of the council of the Stephenson Locomotive Society for several years and editor of its journal in the 1940s. Also a member of the Railway Correspondence and Travel Society, he constantly provided much useful information and photographs for many of its valuable locomotive histories. Although not a modeller himself, he was frequently called upon as an adviser by the Model Railway Club. He was a much respected member of the exclusive Railway Photographic Society.

For valuable assistance during the preparation of this book, my acknowledgements and thanks go especially to Graham Stacey and Bob Ratcliffe of the LCGB; to Real Photographs Company for their skilful printing of difficult negatives and plates; and to the Information and Public Relations Department of the Peninsular & Oriental Steam Navigation Company. Nor must I forget dear Marjorie Nunn who has always talked so freely and engagingly about her husband.

Patrick Russell
March 1980.

1898-1918

Above: Churchward GWR non-superheater 'Star' class 4-6-0 No 4028 King John *enters Paddington station on 27 August 1910, at the end of its 225-mile non-stop journey from Plymouth with the 8.30am Dining Car express. The booked time of just over four hours with a load of 300 ton or more was well within the capability of these powerful new four-cylinder locomotives. Indeed the initial three batches of 10 built in 1907-09 were at first unsuperheated, although this was changed within a few years. When the 'King' class was introduced in 1927 No 4028 changed its name to* Roumanian Monarch, *which it kept until 1940. It was withdrawn from service in November 1951.*

Left: Deep in the Thames Valley countryside at Bourne End, junction for Great Marlow, on a bright spring morning in April 1900 City-bound commuters, top hats, tail coats and all, have been awaiting the arrival from High Wycombe of the 9.1am through train to Paddington via Maidenhead. It is just pulling in behind one of the old GWR 'Queen' class 2-2-2 singles, which had been introduced at Swindon in 1873 during the period of Joseph Armstrong's superintendence, and were now nearing the end of their active lives. The 'New Line' from High Wycombe to London via Gerrard's Cross was not opened until 1906.

Below left: Britain's first Pacific locomotive was also the GWR's only example of this type. Churchward's four-cylinder 4-6-2 No 111 The Great Bear *could regularly be seen taking the 6.30pm Bristol Dining Car express out of Paddington, as on this occasion on 24 August 1910. Completed at Swindon in January 1908, it was always a poor performer, and restricted by weight to this particular route, usually sneaking back under cover of darkness with a fast freight. When a new boiler was needed in 1924, all concerned had had enough and Churchward's successor, C. B. Collett, had it dismantled and replaced by a 'Castle' class 4-6-0 with the same number but a change of name to* Viscount Churchill.

Below: De Glehn-du Bousquet four-cylinder compound Atlantic 4-4-2 No 102 La France *poses in the autumn sunshine at Westbourne Park shed shortly after its arrival from France in October 1903. It was built by the Société Alsacienne des Constructions Mécaniques at Belfort and purchased by the GWR on the instigation of G. J. Churchward, whose fascination with the superb engineering prompted his famous remark: 'This is watchmakers' work'. Two slightly larger versions followed from the same source in 1905, and all three subsequently received Swindon standard boilers. They lasted until the mid-1920s, latterly working from Oxford.*

Above: Opportunities for seeing one of Patrick Stirling's renowned GNR 8ft bogie singles on top link express work were becoming rather rare by 13 September 1902, when 4-2-2 No 668 appeared at the head of the 2pm Kings Cross to Doncaster speeding north through Hatfield. Built at Doncaster in 1882, it was this locomotive which covered the 105 miles to Grantham in 101min to give a flying start to the East Coast route's success on that exciting final night of the celebrated 'Race to Aberdeen' on 21 August 1895. Altogether 53 were constructed with modifications over a 25-year period from 1870, and later Ivatt rebuilt some of them with his standard domed boiler. All were scrapped by 1916 save for the original engine No 1, which was restored for preservation and subsequent appearance in both the Centenary and Rail 150 cavalcades.

Below: Having just passed Ganwick box GNR superheated Class K1 0-8-0 No 454 approaches Hadley Wood North Tunnel with an up through coal train on 19 April 1913. This was one of H. A. Ivatt's large mineral engines, which were aptly nicknamed 'Long Toms' and are particularly remembered for the loud bark of their exhaust. It was included in a supplementary batch of five built at Doncaster in 1909 that differed from the first 50 engines, although later joined by some rebuilds, in having larger cylinders, piston valves and reduced boiler pressure. As LNER Class Q2 they became extinct in 1935.

Left: Assuredly those hats were not part of standard GNR regulation issue, although it must have been very hot work shunting in the yard at Hitchin on 5 July 1902, as the men discuss the next operation for old 251 class 2-4-0 No 258. As seen here it has lost its dome on rebuilding by Stirling, but the 10 mixed traffic engines of this class, having outside frames and bearings and 6ft coupled wheels, were a product of the last year of Sturrock's regime, built by Sharp Stewart as long ago as 1866.

Below: Stirling GNR Class G2 0-4-4WT No 624 of 1878 bustles into Finsbury Park with a local suburban train bound for High Barnet around the turn of the century. There were 46 of these engines built at Doncaster between 1872 and 1881, and many were fitted with condensing apparatus for working over the Metropolitan lines to Moorgate. All had been replaced on these services by about 1910, and the survivors transferred away. The class was extinct by 1921 apart from one used as a crane engine at Doncaster Works until 1928.

Right: GER Class S46 4-4-0 No 1891 slogs its way up the formidable Brentwood bank on 7 August 1909, with the 12.38pm holiday extra express from Liverpool Street to Lowestoft. This was one of James Holden's celebrated 'Claud Hamiltons' from the first series of 10 engines which closely followed the prototype out of Stratford Works in 1900. They could be distinguished by the low pitched cab roof small round topped tender. In 1916 it was rebuilt with superheated Belpaire boiler, and then in 1932 received an extended smokebox which took it into LNER Class D15/2. It was scrapped in this condition in 1952.

Below: This is indeed a rare view of James Holden's remarkable three-cylinder Class A55 'Decapod' 0-10-0T No 20 and shows it preparing at Brentwood for a trial trip on 29 March 1903. Capable of rapid acceleration, it was built as a response to early proposals for electrification of the extensive GER London suburban system. It was then the most powerful locomotive in the world and in concept years ahead of its time, but unfortunately its excessive weight proved self-defeating and in 1906 it was converted into a two-cylinder 0-8-0 tender engine. In this condition it compared unfavourably with the latest 0-6-0 goods engines of Class G58, and was scrapped in 1913.

Above: Running into Norwich Thorpe with the 8.6am train from Kings Lynn to Yarmouth Vauxhall on 15 April 1911, comes one of the last few GER 'Little Sharpie' 2-4-0s to remain in service. This was No 30, which had been among the first four delivered by Sharp Stewart back in 1867, when it was No 26. Altogether there were 40 of these popular Johnson engines of the No 1 class built between 1867-72, 10 at Stratford and the remainder by Sharp Stewart. All were rebuilt by James Holden around 1890 with longer cabs and coupled wheels increased to 5ft 8in, while the dome was pitched well forward on the boiler. Scrapping had begun in 1901, but the final engine to go in December 1913 was in fact the original No 1.

Left: GER Class G69 2-4-2T No 70 with an enormous rake of suburban four-wheelers pulls strongly past the Squirrels Heath (now Gidea Park) distant signal near the end of its journey with the 11.36am from Liverpool Street on 2 November 1912. Known as 'Glasshouse Gobblers', 20 were built at Stratford in 1911-12 as a final development by S. D. Holden of the Great Eastern radial tank engine. They were clearly distinguishable in original condition by their high-arched cabs with side windows, straight brass-rimmed chimneys and four-columned safety valves. They were also fitted with condensing apparatus for London suburban work until later banished to rural branches, where they survived to the late 1950s as LNER Class F6.

Left: Special through coal train arrives at Aldersbrook sidings from Peterborough on 8 July 1911, in charge of GER Class G58 0-6-0 No 1229, built at Stratford in 1906. This was another James Holden design, dating from 1902, which was developed from his Class F48 of two years earlier, having larger boiler and Belpaire firebox. The boilers and cylinders of both classes were interchangeable with the equivalent 'Claud Hamilton' passenger engines. Eventually the earlier class was converted and all were superheated, which made a total of 90 engines forming LNER Class J17. The last survivors were taken out of service in September 1962, but one which was superheated by the LNER in 1923 has been preserved in those colours as No 1217E.

Below: Struggling up Brentwood bank, GER Class N31 0-6-0 No 947 has just cleared the station, and attacks the last mile to the summit at Ingrave with a special fast goods train bound for Parkeston on 13 May 1911. These small six-coupled goods engines were first brought out by James Holden in 1893. Of similar size and appearance to T. W. Worsdell's Class Y14s of 1883, they were never the equal of their highly successful predecessors, and proved to be sluggish performers known sarcastically as 'The Swifts'. This engine was built at Stratford in 1897 and only lasted until 1914. Indeed only 18 of the original 82 survived to become LNER Class J14, and all were withdrawn by April 1925.

Above: One smartly dressed young lady seems to be the solitary passenger aboard the 1.15pm train about to leave Corringham on 16 June 1909, for the short 2¼-mile journey to Kynochtown, which has been known as Coryton since 1921. This was the Corringham Light Railway, which linked these two villages across the marshes on the north side of the Thames basin east of Tilbury. It served the industrial works at Shellhaven, and also made connection with the LT&SR branch to Thames Haven. The 0-4-2T locomotive Kynite was supplied by Kerr Stuart for the opening in 1901 along with the strange, partially open-sided bogie coach. Kynite was scrapped before World War II, but the railway itself did not close until March 1952.

Right: Colne Valley & Halstead Railway 0-6-2T No 5 has just arrived at Halstead with the 12.20pm goods train from Haverhill to Chappel on 6 August 1909. Still almost new, it had been built by Hudswell Clarke only the previous year mainly to handle the extensive local brick traffic. It was the largest and most powerful of the five locomotives taken into LNER stock when the line was absorbed on 1 July 1923. As Class N18 No 8314 it was transferred to shunting duties at Colchester until withdrawn at the beginning of 1928.

Above: The Peninsular & Oriental Steam Navigation Company's liner SS Persia arrives at Tilbury with a tug escort on 26 March 1910, at the end of its voyage from Bombay. Built by Caird & Company of Greenock and commissioned in October 1900, it was the fifth and last of the P&O's 'Egypt' class single-screw passenger liners with a gross tonnage of 7,951, and was employed on the mail services to India and Australia. On 30 December 1915, this fine ship was torpedoed in the Mediterranean 70 miles south-east of Crete by the German submarine U-38, and sank rapidly with the loss of 334 lives. As much as 30 hours later the 167 survivors were picked up by a trawler and landed at Alexandria. The sinking was considered one of the worst atrocities of World War I, which did much to influence neutral, especially American, opinion against Germany.

Left: London, Tilbury & Southend Railway 1 class 4-4-2T No 8 Rainham *bowls along in open country near East Horndon at the head of an elderly set of four-wheelers dating from 1877 which form the 9.15am local train from Southend to Upminster on 23 March 1910. Built by Sharp Stewart in 1880, it belonged to the original series of Tilbury tanks introduced when that company first began to use its own motive power. Previously this had been provided by the GER, and although never officially attributed to him these engines were undoubtedly the work of William Adams, who had been locomotive superintendent of the GER until 1878.*

Below: Coming from the opposite direction Midland Railway 2-4-0 No 170 enters Upminster station with a boat train special from St Pancras to Southend to connect with the sailing of the PS Kingfisher *on 10 August 1908. Johnson designed four series of progressively larger 2-4-0s before concentrating on bogie passenger engines after 1882. This one belonged to the second series of 40 6ft 6in engines of this type, and was included among the 30 which were built by Dubs & Co between 1876-80. Although it was not until 1 January 1912, that the Midland absorbed the LT&SR, it had long enjoyed running powers over this line since 1894 when the connection from South Tottenham to Forest Gate was completed.*

Above: A North London Railway suburban train working over the Great Northern main line was once a familiar enough sight, having commenced as long ago as 1875. The 2.18pm Saturdays only Broad Street to Potters Bar, formed of a typical set of the older, close-coupled four-wheeled stock, emerges from Hadley Wood North Tunnel on 19 April 1913, behind Park outside cylinder 4-4-0T No 39. Altogether 74 of these sturdy locomotives were constructed at the company's Bow Works up to 1907, many of which were rebuilds from William Adams' original design of 1868. All were taken first into LNWR and then LMS stock at the Grouping, but withdrawal thereafter was fairly rapid and complete by 1929.

Below: Dwarfed by Clayton's imposing clerestory stock, Midland Railway 115 class 4-2-2 No 118 sweeps through Cricklewood at the head of the 5.3pm express from St Pancras to Derby and Manchester on 6 June 1903. This handsome 7ft 9in Johnson 'Spinner' belonged to the penultimate series of 15 engines built at Derby in 1896-99, and was allocated to Kentish Town shed at this time. When withdrawn by the LMS in 1928 as No 673, it had become the last of all the Midland's 95 bogie singles to remain in service. It was restored to its former Midland colours, and kept in immaculate condition at Derby Works. Later it was moved to the Midland Railway Centre at Butterley, whence it emerged in 1980 to take an honoured place in the Rocket 150 cavalcade at Rainhill.

Above: More than a decade before the electric suburban lines to Watford were constructed alongside, Webb LNWR 'Precedent' class 2-4-0 No 955 Charles Dickens *speeds north through Harrow & Wealdstone with the down 4pm Euston to Manchester express on 31 May 1902. On emerging from Crewe in 1882 it was the last of the original 6ft 6in engines which were equipped with Allan straight-link motion. After 1893 the class was progressively renewed to conform with the earlier Ramsbottom 'Newtons' which had been rebuilt as improved 'Precedents' from 1887, so that by 1901 the total of these larger 'Jumbos' had grown to 166. This particular engine put in a phenomenal amount of work, averaging 100,000 miles per annum for its first 20 years, which must have worn it out for it was a comparatively early casualty when withdrawn in 1912.*

Right: Old Beyer Peacock Metropolitan Railway A class 4-4-0T No 2, from the original batch of 18 engines delivered in 1864, steams past the camera bearing an unlikely Willesden destination board in this interesting view near South Harrow on 5 September 1898. It shows the short-lived Ealing & South Harrow Railway still in the final stages of construction. The line was built to connect with the District Railway at Hanger Lane, and was ready for traffic the following year but no passenger trains were operated. Taken over by the District in 1900, it was chosen as that company's first line for electrification and opened from Mill Hill Park (now Acton Town) in June 1903.

Above: The lightly loaded 6.50am from Marylebone, known as 'The Pady' in the hunting country which it served, arrives at Whetstone for the last stop on its all stations journey to Leicester on 26 March 1910. The divergence of the tracks to accommodate a single island platform was a typical feature of stations on the GCR London Extension. The engine is Robinson Class 8F 4-6-0 No 1100, one of 10 built by Beyer Peacock in 1906 for fast goods traffic. Better known as the 'Immingham' class after the only one of their number to be named, these 6ft 6in engines with graceful curved splashers became LNER Class B4.

Below: The handsome lines of GCR locomotives were not confined to the Robinson regime as witness this immaculate Parker Class 2A 4-4-0 No 690, ready to leave Neasden shed on 4 June 1904. The London Extension had opened in 1899 and was still something of a novelty at the time this photograph was taken. The engine will be making the five-mile journey back to Marylebone to pick up the 6.5pm stopping train to Leicester. It was one of six built at Gorton in 1894 by the then Manchester, Sheffield & Lincolnshire Railway supplementing the 25 earlier engines of Class 2, all of which survived the Grouping in 1923 to form LNER Class D7.

Above: LCDR F class 2-4-0T No 63 stands in Victoria station on empty stock working in the last year of that company's separate existence before merger with the South Eastern Railway to form the SECR on 1 January 1899. Originally known as the 'Second Sondes' class, six of these engines had been built at Longhedge Works in 1865 from designs by William Martley which used boilers and other parts of the useless Crampton 4-4-0STs of 1858. They were extensively rebuilt by Kirtley in 1876-78 and all were eventually withdrawn in 1909.

Right: SECR M3 class 4-4-0 No 485 passes Rochester with an up boat train from Dover Harbour to Victoria on 28 June 1902. The class had been introduced on to the London Chatham & Dover Railway in 1891, and represented the final development of William Kirtley's 4-4-0 types. This engine was among the last three, built at Longhedge Works in 1900-1, which never carried a LCDR number. Easy access to the motion made them distinctively noisy engines which earned them the nickname 'Clatterbangs'. Prematurely eclipsed by Wainwright 4-4-0s and missing out on a superheater rebuild, all 26 of the class were withdrawn between 1925-28.

Above: Wainwright SECR Class D 4-4-0 No 145 opens up vigorously as it passes Hither Green C box with the 3.35pm Charing Cross to Hastings parlour car express on 7 May 1910. Built by Dubs & Co in 1903, it was at this time one of four allocated to Hastings to cover the heavily loaded business trains over this difficult route. The job was rather too much for them, especially with the weighty new clerestory type stock seen here, and they were replaced in 1914 by the new, larger Class L 4-4-0s. Many of them were later transformed on rebuilding by Maunsell with new superheated boilers, becoming Class D1. No 145 was so dealt with at Ashford in 1922, and thereafter put in almost 40 years more service.

Above: On one of the celebrated Colonel Stephens' railways, the standard gauge Hundred of Manhood & Selsey Tramway, Manning Wardle 0-6-0ST No 2 Sidlesham *is shunting stock alongside the locomotive shed at Selsey on 15 April 1911. Built in 1861, it had been purchased from Blagdon Waterworks near Bristol in 1907, and was scrapped in 1932 shortly before the railway closed completely in January 1935. This eight-mile line connecting Selsey with the LBSCR station at Chichester had opened in 1897, but even a change of name to the West Sussex Railway in 1924 did not arrest its steady decline after World War I.*

Below: On the 3ft gauge Rye & Camber Tramway the well-filled 2.10pm train to Camber Sands on 18 July 1914, is just leaving Rye behind Victoria, *the second and largest of the two Bagnall 2-4-0Ts supplied in 1895 and 1897. Also owned by Colonel Stephens, this line was opened for two miles to Rye Golf Links in 1895 and extended a further half mile to Camber Sands in 1908. Both steam engines were eventually displaced by a petrol locomotive acquired in 1925, and were sold off long before the line was taken over by the Admiralty in 1940.*

Above: Portsmouth-based LBSCR Class B2X 4-4-0 No 322 blows off hard whilst passing Balham Intermediate box on a filling in turn to Norwood with a gas tank train from Battersea yard on 28 September 1912. It had been rebuilt with larger boiler by Marsh in 1908 from one of Robert Billinton's poor steaming Class B2 engines introduced in 1895, which were known as 'Grasshoppers' because of their strange riding characteristics. Although useful for much secondary work the rebuilds were still inferior to the later 4-4-0s of Class B4 and B4X, and all 25 engines were withdrawn between 1929-33.

Above right: Standing in East Croydon station at the head of an up Tunbridge Wells West to Victoria train on 22 June 1912, is LBSCR Class E5 0-6-2T No 591 Tillington. This was one of Robert Billinton's third series of radial tanks of which 30 were built at Brighton between 1902-04. Based at New Cross for many years, it was the last to retain its name as well as the old yellow livery until as late as 1917. When new it had operated the 'Grande Vitesse' van trains between London Bridge and Newhaven Harbour which survived until 1906, many years after the deepening of the harbour had rendered this former tidal service obsolete.

Right: Making one of the proudest sights on the LBSCR, Marsh Class H2 4-4-2 No 422 gathers speed past Purley at the head of the 1.55pm Victoria-Brighton Pullman Car express on 7 September 1912. Turned out at Brighton Works in July 1911, it belonged to the second series of six superheated Atlantics which followed the earlier five saturated engines of Class H1 built in 1905-06, and was stationed at Battersea at this time for working the best express services. Only after passing into Southern Railway ownership did these engines receive names, and No 422B became North Foreland in 1925. It was ultimately withdrawn after sustaining a broken left cylinder at East Croydon in August 1956.

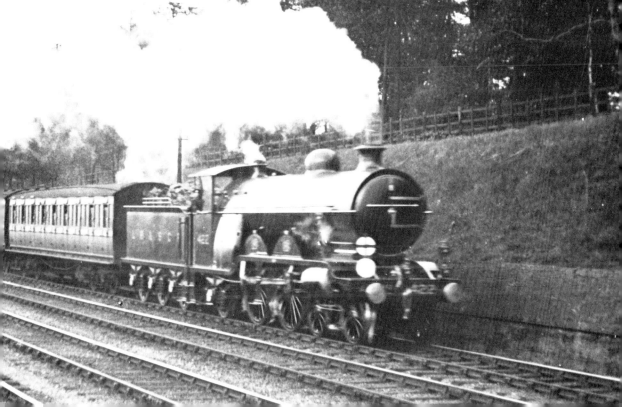

Above: LSWR F13 class four-cylinder 4-6-0 No 334 pulls out of Salisbury yard with the 11.15am heavy goods train for Southampton Docks on 18 April 1914. Dugald Drummond's first 4-6-0 design, this was the last of five engines built at Nine Elms Works in 1905, probably the worst of their type ever seen in Britain. With poor steaming, clumsy positioning of the outside cylinders and lubrication problems, it is hard to believe that such feeble performers could come from the same stable as the legendary Class T9s. Intended for the West of England main line expresses to Exeter, all were relegated within a year to freight and secondary working. An unsuccessful attempt at improvement was made in 1920 when No 333 was rebuilt by Urie with extended smokebox and superheater. They were all withdrawn in 1924, and then under Maunsell entirely reconstructed as two-cylinder mixed traffic 4-6-0s in the pattern of Urie's H15 class.

Below: Although not displaying quite the correct head signals, LSWR 135 class 4-4-0 No 138 was shortly due to leave Bournemouth West with a stopping train to Brockenhurst and Southampton on 24 November 1900. This type was the first of Adams' express passenger engines for the South Western, and 12 were ordered from Beyer Peacock in 1880. No 138 appears to have been rather accident prone and was involved in at least four minor mishaps in its earlier years. It was included among seven of the class summarily withdrawn at the end of 1913, the remainder going at intervals up to 1924.

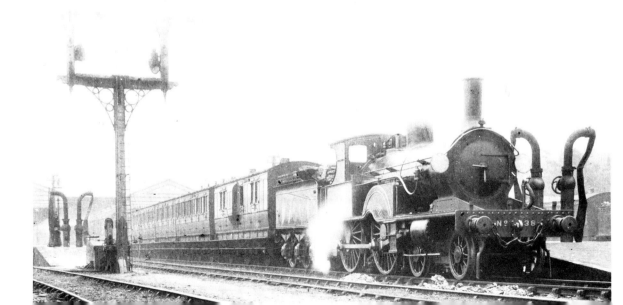

Top: Outside Moorswater shed on the Liskeard & Looe Railway about 1902 old long-boilered 0-6-0ST Cheesewring is ready to drop its fire for the night. This locomotive had been bought from Gilkes Wilson of Middlesbrough in 1864 by the Liskeard & Caradon Railway, but with its affairs in the hands of a receiver both stock and working were taken over by the Liskeard & Looe in 1901. When both companies were absorbed by the GWR on 1 January 1909, it became No 1311 and was surprisingly posted to Old Oak Common during World War I, where it evoked much curiosity before being scrapped in 1919.

Above: Dean GWR double-framed 'Aberdare' class 2-6-0 No 2666 picks up water from Goring troughs as it hurries along with an express goods from London to Banbury via Oxford on 13 March 1915. This engine had been built at Swindon in 1902, and like all the later members of the class had received a Standard No 4 boiler from the outset. It had been superheated in 1910, and was among the first withdrawals in 1934 when replaced by newly converted 2-8-2Ts of the 7200 class. Essentially a goods version of the well known 'Bulldog' 4-4-0s, they were at first allocated to working on Aberdare to Swindon coal trains from which they derived their name.

Above: Brecon & Merthyr Railway double-framed 0-6-0ST No 31 Tor has just arrived at Newport with the 7.50pm from Rhymney on 31 July 1905. The southern end of the Brecon & Merthyr line finished at Bassaleg and the company had running powers thence over the three miles into the GWR station at Newport. Tor and Allt were two similar engines, designed by Henry Appleby and built by the Avonside Engine Co in 1874, which had been bought from the Neath & Brecon Railway in 1877. They were used for both goods and passenger work on the Rhymney line for many years until withdrawn at the end of 1921.

Below: Taff Vale Railway Class U 0-6-2T No 194 is in charge of the 2.10pm suburban train from Penarth on 11 August 1913. Just leaving Riverside, which later became part of Cardiff General station, it has a short remaining journey to the GWR terminus at Clarence Road near the Docks. Eight of these Riches designed engines were built by the Vulcan Foundry in 1895, and together with seven of the similar Class U1 handled the main line passenger traffic so well that they were called the 'high flyers'. Relegated on the advent of Cameron's big Class A 0-6-2Ts in 1914, all were later rebuilt and survived to be taken into GWR stock in 1922. The last withdrawal was in 1931, although one engine found its way into NCB ownership at Granville Colliery and was not cut up until 1954.

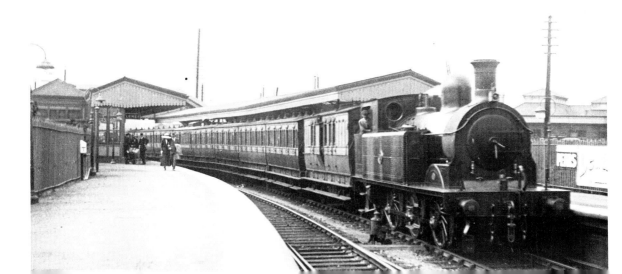

Top: Shed staff at Machynlleth line up to be photographed with Cambrian Railways 'Small Passenger' class 2-4-0 No 28 on 29 June 1909. This engine belonged to a standard Sharp Stewart design, and was originally built as long ago as 1863. It was the first among 12 of this class bought by the Cambrian, and was formerly named Mazeppa. They had been employed on the main line passenger traffic for nearly 30 years, but by this time No 28 had been transferred to surplus stock, and although assisting trains up Talerddig bank was regarded as pretty useless. Even so it was not finally withdrawn until December 1920.

Above: On the 1ft 11¼in gauge Vale of Rheidol Light Railway the 3pm train to Devil's Bridge is setting out from Aberystwyth on 13 August 1913, behind Festiniog Railway 0-4-0ST No 4 Palmerston. For three successive years immediately before World War I and again in 1921 and 1922, it had been loaned together with a driver to help out with the peak summer traffic, when Territorial Army units were encamped down in the valley. This ancient locomotive with its separate tender was one of four supplied by George England in 1863, and indeed No 2 Prince survives to this day on the Festiniog Railway. Palmerston's demise came during World War II when it had been reduced to driving a steam hammer at the Boston Lodge Works.

Above: Midland & South Western Junction Railway 4-4-0 No 8 crosses over the LSWR main line to reach the M&SW platform at Andover Junction on 7 August 1913 with the 1.52pm 'North Express' from Southampton West to Cheltenham, conveying through coach for Birmingham. There were nine of these locomotives designed by former engine driver, James Tyrrell, and all were built by the NBL Company during the railway's most successful years between 1905 and 1914. They continued to work on the line after it was absorbed into the GWR system in 1923. This engine which dated from 1912 became No 1126 and received a Swindon Standard No 2 taper boiler in 1928. It had outlived the rest of the class when withdrawn in December 1938.

Left: Somerset & Dorset Joint Railway Class C 0-4-4T No 54 is approaching Wells with the 12.15pm train from Glastonbury on 11 April 1914. Four of these efficient Johnson tank engines were supplied by the Vulcan Foundry in 1884, and for some years worked passenger trains on the main line. No 54 was scrapped in 1921, and replaced by a similar engine purchased from the Midland Railway which was given the same number. The short Wells branch of just over five miles, which left the Highbridge line at Glastonbury, had originally been opened as broad gauge in 1859 and was finally closed in October 1951.

Left: Stratford-upon-Avon & Midland Junction Railway 0-6-0 No 07 trundles along with a freight from Blisworth to Stratford on 29 July 1915, near Woodford West Junction, which provided the link with the GCR at Woodford & Hinton. Its Crewe origins are readily apparent, and indeed it was built there in 1863, one of Ramsbottom's celebrated 'Special DX' class of LNWR goods engines of which no less than 943 were constructed over the period 1858-74. Three of them were acquired by the East & West Junction Railway in December 1891 for working Midland goods trains through from Olney to Broom Junction. It was the only one fitted with vacuum brakes, and the last to be withdrawn at the end of 1920.

Below: At Peterborough (GN) on 16 July 1904, a Midland & Great Northern Joint Railway stopping train arrives from South Lynn and Wisbech behind Ivatt Da class 0-6-0 No 84. At this time it was rare to see one of these engines on a passenger turn. They were the GNR Class J5 standard goods design, and in order to relieve a motive power shortage on the M&GN in 1900 it had been necessary to divert 12 of them from the final order for 25 then under contract from Dubs & Co. All were rebuilt with larger 4ft 8in boilers in the 1920s so that when absorbed into LNER stock in 1937 they belonged to Class J3, but to complicate matters nine of them later reverted to their original boiler size of 4ft 5in which took them into LNER Class J4. One had the distinction of being the last surviving M&GN engine when it was condemned in November 1951.

Above: Sacré GCR Class 18 0-6-0 No 327 stands in the up platform of the Great Northern station at Retford waiting to shunt the empty stock of an arrival from Sheffield on 13 April 1903. The class was introduced in 1869 for working goods traffic on the Cheshire Lines of the former Manchester, Sheffield & Lincolnshire Railway, and No 327 was among 45 modified 5ft 3in engines fitted with flush-topped fireboxes which were built at Gorton in 1872-74. They were later reboilered, but all had been scrapped before World War I.

Left: Kirtley Midland Railway double-framed 0-6-0 No 612, seen here as rebuilt by Johnson, heads north through Cudworth on the main line between Sheffield and Leeds with an empty coal train on the afternoon of 9 October 1900. Several hundreds of these sturdy, long-lived engines were built from 1863-74, and used extensively on the London coal traffic and much else besides for many years. Latterly, when merged with the rebuilds from the earlier straight-framed series dating from 1852, they could be distinguished by the curved running plate over their coupling-rod cranks. Four survived into Nationalisation, and the very last to go was 82 years old when withdrawn in 1951 as BR No 58110.

Below: Hull & Barnsley Railway 6ft 2-4-0 No 38 relaxes at Springhead shed on 19 September 1904, before taking out an afternoon train to Cudworth. Ten of these engines were constructed in 1885 by Beyer Peacock to the designs of William Kirtley for the opening of the main line from Hull Cannon Street, and until 1910 they were the only passenger locomotives the company possessed. In 1900 five of them including this one were rebuilt by Matthew Stirling with larger cylinders and domeless boiler. All had been scrapped by 1922 when the railway was merged with the NER.

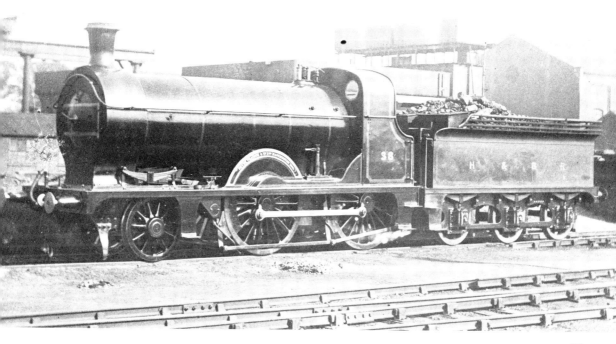

Top: Beyer Peacock 0-6-4T No 1 The Major, built in 1885, relaxes at the Rock Ferry terminus of the Mersey Railway on 14 August 1902, until time for the short return trip under the river to Liverpool Central. It was named after an enterprising Victorian entrepreneur, Major Samuel Isaac, who had backed construction of the infamous tunnel beneath the Mersey. In steam days, even though locomotives were fitted with condensing gear, the steep descents from either side made for the most foul conditions below. Early electrification of the line was completed in the following year, and all the steam engines sold except for The Major, which was retained until 1907 and then scrapped. Another of the class, No 5 Cecil Raikes, had worked at Shipley Collieries until 1953 and has been preserved in Liverpool Museum.

Above: Across at Liverpool Exchange on the Lancashire Yorkshire Railway the following day, 15 August 1902, one of the dwindling number of Barton Wright 6ft 4-4-0s, No 890, has just used the turntable in readiness for a return working to Preston. Altogether 110 of these engines had been supplied by various makers during the period 1880-87. This one had been completed at the end of 1885 by the Vulcan Foundry, and like most of the class, was destined for a comparatively short life, being withdrawn just three years after this photograph was taken. They were made steadily obsolete by superior Aspinall engines turned out by the new Horwich Works after 1889, although two at Newton Heath shed survived until 1930, outlasting any other by at least 17 years.

Top: With noticeably little effort Bowen-Cooke four-cylinder 'Claughton' class 4-6-0 No 650 Lord Rathmore pulls out of Carlisle for the south with the 8.30am express for Euston on 28 June 1915. Completed at Crewe in June 1913, it was among the first 10 engines of this final flowering of LNWR express passenger motive power which totalled 130 locomotives by 1921. Victims of the management politics which accompanied the formation of the LMSR, they never really achieved their full potential. Under H. P. M. Beames' supervision 20 were rebuilt in 1928 with larger Belpaire boilers, 10 having Caprotti valve gear. Between 1930-33 a further 42, including Lord Rathmore, were withdrawn and replaced by new three-cylinder 'Patriot' class 4-6-0s designed by Sir Henry Fowler.

Above: Furness Railway Class D1 0-6-0 No 116 drifts along towards Carnforth with a goods train from Barrow Docks on 30 July 1912. A total of 55 ensured that these engines formed the largest single class on the railway. Of typical Sharp Stewart provenance, they were delivered at intervals over the period 1866-83. No 116 dated from 1881, and under W. F. Pettigrew's superintendence in 1901 it had received a larger steel boiler with Rumsbottom safety valves as well as an improved cab. It was among a few that survived to be taken into LMS ownership, but was scrapped soon afterwards in 1925. It is perhaps an intriguing thought that another of the class, No 115, may still exist in original condition, albeit some 200ft underground submerged in the mining subsidence at Lindal in October 1892.

Left: Built to serve the northern end of the West Cumberland coalfields, the Maryport & Carlisle Railway was the smallest of the seven pre-Grouping companies to use the great Citadel station at Carlisle. The 1.25pm train from Whitehaven is just arriving on 31 July 1912, in charge of 2-4-0 No 10, which had been constructed at the company's works at Maryport in 1878. Seen here after being twice rebuilt, its long period of service was to take it into LMS stock in 1923 for its final two years. Three of these engines, together with some 0-4-2s, were Hugh Smellie's last contribution to the M&C locomotive stock before departing to take up a similar appointment with the G&SWR at Kilmarnock.

Below: Two young admirers take an enviable look at the almost new Reid NBR Class I 4-4-2 No 906 Teribus, which is about to leave Carlisle with the 2.45pm stopping train to Hawick and Edinburgh on 31 July 1912. Based at Carlisle for its first 20 years, this locomotive was the last of six built by Robert Stephenson & Co in 1911, which were slightly heavier than the initial 14 engines dating from 1906. None of this later series were superheated before the Grouping and they became LNER Class C10, but after receiving this modification they were merged with the remainder, which by then included two more added in 1921, under Class C11. Unfortunately, the rise of the Pacific type rendered Atlantics generally early victims of obsolescence, and these fine engines had all gone by 1939.

Top: This scene at Kilmarnock on 7 August 1899, shows two of James Stirling's G&SWR 6 class 7ft 1in 4-4-0s still in original condition complete with Ramsbottom safety valves. No 44A is arriving on a local train from Glasgow, whilst No 36A simmers in the yard beyond. When introduced in 1873 these engines with inside frames and cylinders were only the second of their type in the country after Wheatley's 224 class for the NBR. Of the original 22, six had been withdrawn in 1895-96, whilst the remainder were transferred to the duplicate list. Between 1899 and 1901 Manson set about rebuilding the latter with new boilers, modernised cabs and closed splashers. This took them well into the LMS era, when they could still be seen working trains to the Clyde coast.

Above: The 9.30am through express from Manchester enters Glasgow St Enoch station on 1 August 1911, behind G&SWR 240 class 4-4-0 No 251. This class consisted of 15 engines designed by Manson and built at Kilmarnock in 1904-06. They were identical in most respects with his fine 8 class engines dating from 1892, but they incorporated a much-needed larger boiler with increased working pressure and a higher cab. Sandwiched between the leading Midland clerestory vehicles is the obligatory Lancashire & Yorkshire coach demanded in acknowledgement of running powers granted over its metals as far as Hellifield.

Above: NBR Class K 4-4-0 No 322 emerges from the Mound Tunnel as it pulls strongly away from Waverley station with the 3.12pm Edinburgh-Aberdeen express on 20 September 1910, conveying through GNSR coach next to the tender. The 12 6ft 6in engines of this class were all completed at Cowlairs in 1903, and proved to be Matthew Holmes' last design. In their day they were capable of handling the heaviest expresses over this road, usually being well able to hold their own alongside the later Reid 4-4-0s and Atlantics. However, they were never superheated and three were scrapped before the Grouping, whilst the remainder formed LNER Class D26 before becoming extinct in 1926.

Left: A quartet of NER express passenger locomotives must have been a treat for young locospotters, as they paraded through Princes Street Gardens, Edinburgh, on their way down from Haymarket shed to Waverley station to take up southbound workings on the evening of 20 September 1910. All are Wilson Worsdell engines, led by Class R 4-4-0 No 1236 built at Gateshead in 1907, followed by two of the slightly modified two-cylinder Atlantic 4-4-2s of Class V/09 Nos 703 and 698 both only weeks out of Darlington Works, and finally the second of the original Class V Atlantics No 649 which had emerged from Gateshead at the end of 1903. All were unsuperheated at this date.

Above: McDonnell NER Class 38 4-4-0 No 234 reposes inside Neville Hill shed, Leeds, around 1904. It was built at Gateshead in 1884, but in this view has since received a Worsdell boiler and chimney. Product of a brief and unpopular reign at Gateshead for this capable locomotive superintendent from Ireland's Great Southern & Western Railway, the 28 engines of this class never proved as powerful or free-running as the earlier Fletcher 901 class 2-4-0s beside which the enginemen so unfavourably compared them. Nevertheless they became useful performers on the less demanding passenger turns, and the last four did not go until the end of 1920.

Below: Soon after leaving Newcastle NER Class S 4-6-0 No 740 storms past Low Fell to begin the climb to Chester-le-Street and Durham on its way south with a fast freight bound for Hull on 14 May 1910. Ironically they were the first passenger locomotives of the 4-6-0 type in the country when introduced by Wilson Worsdell in 1899, but this engine was among the second batch of 10 built at Gateshead in 1906. No 2006 of the original group had appeared at the Paris Exhibition in 1900 where it won the Grand Prize and gold medal. Their performance on the road however, was disappointing by comparison with the contemporary Class R 4-4-0s and Class V Atlantics. All 40 were withdrawn by 1938, but No 761 was retained as a counter pressure test locomotive first at Darlington and then at Rugby until 1951.

Left: Railwaymen crowd the end of the platform at Gateshead to greet the LNWR Royal Train hauled by the resplendent NER Class V 4-4-2 No 1792 as it comes off the High Level Bridge across the Tyne at Newcastle on 12 July 1906, following the opening by His Majesty of the new King Edward VII Bridge some 800 yards up the river. The Gateshead Works' photographer may also be noted obtaining his record of the occasion. The engine was one of the original two-cylinder unsuperheated Atlantics designed by Wilson Worsdell and built at Gateshead in 1904.

Below: Maunsell succeeded Coey as locomotive superintendent of the Great Southern & Western in 1911, but after two years he moved on to a similar appointment with the SECR at Ashford. In 1913 there appeared the only passenger locomotive of his reign at Inchicore in the shape of a large new superheated 4-4-0 with Belpaire boiler and inside Walschaerts valve gear, No 341 Sir William Goulding. In this picture it is seen arriving at Cork with the 11am 'Tourists Express' from Dublin on Saturday 25 July 1914. Because of its considerable weight of almost 60 tons it was unpopular with the Civil Engineer's department, and no further examples were built. Apparently not a great success, it was withdrawn in 1928 three years after the Great Southern Railways had been formed.

Left: Great Southern & Western Railway 321 class 4-4-0 No 326 passes the locomotive works at Inchicore on its way out of Dublin with an express for Cork on 21 July 1914. Among several new passenger locomotives of the 4-4-0 type designed by Robert Coey, 12 of these taper-boilered engines were constructed at Inchicore in 1904-06 with the Nos 321 to 332. In 1912 his successor, R.E.L. Maunsell, had fitted the engine seen here with a Schmidt superheater, but this was removed in 1916. Except for Nos 324 to 326 which were scrapped in 1927-28, the remainder of the class were subsequently rebuilt with parallel Belpaire boilers and superheaters to equip them for a further 30 years of service.

Top: Cork, Bandon & South Coast Railway 4-6-0T No 14 arrives back at the Albert Quay terminus in Cork on the evening of 25 July 1914. It had spent the day on a long freight trip to Baltimore over 60 miles away to the far south west of Ireland. Eight of these sturdy engines were built by Beyer Peacock between 1906-20, and all entered Great Southern Railways' stock on the amalgamation in 1925. They proved so satisfactory that five were still in use when the original CB&SC system closed in 1961.

Above: Some 30 miles to the south west of Cork was located the Timoleague & Courtmacsherry Light Railway, which opened in 1891 and extended some nine miles from Ballinascarthy Junction on the CB&SCR's Clonakilty branch to serve these two fishing villages. One of its three very different locomotives at this time was the highly unusual inside cylinder 2-6-0T Argadeen, which was built by Hunslet in 1894 and is here waiting to leave Courtmacsherry with a train on 5 September 1901. The railway was taken over by the GSR in 1925 and passenger services ceased in 1947, but this engine's long career only ended in 1957, just three years before the line itself was closed completely.

Top: Waterford, Limerick & Western Railway 0-4-0ST No 29 is almost ready to leave a busy Limerick station, where everyone it seems wears a bowler hat, with the 2pm stopping train on 3 September 1900. That the clock was already pointing to six minutes past two would be unlikely to have bothered many. Its destination was Limerick Junction, an isolated spot 22 miles distant, which was the major interchange point with the Great Southern & Western main line from Dublin to Cork. Indeed the WL&W was absorbed into that system the following year, together with its 58 surviving locomotives. Built by Sharp Stewart in 1865, No 29 was renumbered 228 but withdrawn shortly afterwards.

Above: Waterford & Central Ireland Railway 2-4-0 No 3 marshals its train of antiquated and reputedly most uncomfortable four-wheelers at Waterford on 5 September 1900, in readiness for the slow 60-mile journey northwards to Maryborough. That place too was a junction with the Dublin-Cork main line, and the date was just four days after this small company had been absorbed into the Great Southern & Western Railway. The 10 engines that were taken over lasted for only a very short time thereafter.

Above: Belfast & Northern Counties Railway Class J 2-4-0T No 25 makes a spectacular start from Belfast York Road in charge of the 9.45am mail train to Londonderry on 16 September 1909. It seems rather a small engine for so important a train, but this was before the direct route avoiding reversal at Greenisland opened in 1934. Generally any available motive power was used to take trains for the Coleraine line over this 6¾-mile section, where the main engine would then couple on to the rear. Beyer Peacock supplied four of these locomotives in 1883 when they were fitted with side tanks as seen here. They were later converted into saddle tanks, but all had disappeared by 1934.

1919-1939

Above: At Dundalk Quay Street station a generous complement of passengers are boarding the 4.45pm train bound for the small port of Greenore at the mouth of Carlingford Lough on 23 May 1924. This scene was on the Dundalk, Newry & Greenore Railway, and the engine was 0-6-0ST No 3 Dundalk which had been built at Crewe for the opening of the railway in 1873. This little company was owned by the LNWR and its successors throughout its existence. The Great Northern Railway (Ireland) worked the line after July 1933, but it was closed at the end of 1951 when BR declined further subsidy. The total locomotive stock was six of these saddle tanks, plainly derived from the Ramsbottom 'Special tanks' of the same period, although they had larger wheels and were constructed to the Irish 5ft 3in standard gauge. No 5 was scrapped in 1928 but the remainder lasted until the end.

Below: Belfast & County Down Railway Class I 4-4-2T No 30 heads up the bank to Neill's Hill soon after leaving Belfast Queen's Quay with the 1.15pm Saturday lunchtime commuter train to Donaghadee on 15 May 1920. It was the original engine in a class of 12 supplied by Beyer Peacock at intervals between 1901 and 1921. Unlike the rather feeble Baltic tanks of 1920 which were restricted to the Bangor line, they handled most of the passenger traffic very efficiently for up to half a century. Except for the busy Bangor line the whole system was closed in 1950, and although efforts were made by the Ulster Transport Authority to find them other work all but one were scrapped in 1956. Happily No 30 was saved for preservation in the Belfast Transport Museum.

Above: On the 3ft gauge County Donegal Railways Joint Committee, the 3.45pm mixed train from Killybegs to Londonderry has just crossed the River Finn and is running into Stranorlar station on 8 May 1920, behind Class 5A 2-6-4T No 2A Strabane. *This was during the period of frequent interference and sabotage suffered by the railway in the civil disturbances following the establishment of the Irish Free State. The locomotive was one of three superheated developments of the earlier Class 5 built by Nasmyth Wilson in 1912 which proved to be the last steam engines delivered to the railway. Renamed* Blanche *in 1928, when it also lost the A suffix to its number, it continued in service until the railway closed at the end of 1959, and was then retained for preservation in the Belfast Transport Museum.*

Below: The coastal resort of Ballycastle lying in the north east corner of Co Antrim was linked to the Belfast & Northern Counties Railway main line at Ballymoney by the 16¼-mile 3ft gauge Ballycastle Railway. The 3.20pm train from Ballycastle is just entering its own bay platform at Ballymoney station on 6 May 1920, behind 0-6-0ST No 2 Countess of Antrim. *Three of these engines were delivered by Black Hawthorn for the opening of the railway in 1880. The slightly smaller No 3 was scrapped in 1908 when two new 4-4-2Ts arrived, but the others continued until 1925. The line lost its independence in 1924 when taken over in a rather run down condition by the Northern Counties Committee, but somehow it avoided closure until July 1950.*

Top: Just 15 miles from Ballycastle across the Mull of Kintyre lies the remote Kintyre peninsula of south-west Scotland, astride of which for six miles ran the 2ft 3in gauge Campbeltown & Macrihanish Light Railway. Opened in stages from Campbeltown in 1877, it did not operate a passenger service until the line was completed to Macrihanish in 1906. At Campbeltown shed on 27 April 1922, are two of its locomotives, both built by Andrew Barclay. On the left is the 0-6-2T Argyll of 1906, and to the right the small 0-4-2ST Chevalier of 1885, which was originally a 0-4-0T and had been used for the much earlier mineral workings. The line was closed in September 1931.

Above: On the 3ft gauge Isle of Man Railway Beyer Peacock 2-4-0Ts No 3 Pender and No 10 G. H. Wood vigorously attack the climb away from Douglas, double-heading the 2.25pm train for Port Erin on 18 April 1919. Pender has been delivered for the opening of the railway in 1873, and still retains its sloping smokebox door and Salter safety valves on the bell-shaped dome. G. H. Wood was the first to have enlarged boiler and tank capacity when it arrived in 1905. Despite valiant efforts to preserve the railway as a tourist attraction, all that remains since 1975 of the original system is the 5½-mile section from Castletown to Port Erin.

Right: Train ascending the 2ft 7½in gauge Snowdon Mountain Railway is the 1.30pm from Llanberis on 13 September 1934, approaching the passing loop at Clogwyn three quarters of the way to the summit. The well-filled bogie coach in original open condition with only canvas screens for protection is propelled by one of the Swiss built 0-4-2Ts No 4 Snowdon. *Rising to 3,540ft this is the only rack railway in the British Isles, and it began inauspiciously with a serious accident on the opening day in 1896 when engine No 1 was blown over in a gale and destroyed. Reopening the following year, it has remained a major tourist attraction to this day.*

Below: Rustic scene on the 2ft 4¼in gauge Glyn Valley Tramway shows 0-4-2T No 1 Dennis *apparently making its way through the long grass soon after leaving Chirk with the 10am mixed train to Glynceiriog on 10 July 1919. It was one of two engines of this type supplied by Beyer Peacock when the earlier 1874 horse-drawn tramway was superseded by steam in 1888, and a third arrived in 1892. The line extended 6¼ miles westwards into Denbighshire from the GWR station at Chirk to serve local granite quarries. It was closed completely in July 1935, and the locomotives were scrapped a year later.*

Above: At Craven Arms alongside the GWR Hereford to Shrewsbury main line, Bishop's Castle Railway 0-4-2T No 1 is busy marshalling the 3.10pm mixed train to Bishop's Castle in pouring rain on 30 June 1919. From its opening in 1866 this 10¼-mile standard gauge railway contrived an almost permanently insolvent existence. Original plans for a line to Montgomery did not materialise, and this necessitated reversal at Lydham Heath to reach Bishop's Castle. Engine No 1 was first built in 1869 and acquired from the GWR in 1905. Together with an ancient Kitson 0-6-0 they were the only motive power of the railway's last 30 years, and both were scrapped shortly after its closure in 1935.

Below: Another mixed train, this time on the Cleobury Mortimer & Ditton Priors Light Railway, forms the 9.15am from Cleobury Mortimer on 1 May 1920. It has just arrived at Ditton Priors, where the 0-6-0ST Cleobury promptly takes water. Two of these engines were supplied by Manning Wardle in 1908 for the opening of the 12½-mile line. The railway was absorbed by the GWR on 1 January 1922, and both engines were subsequently rebuilt as pannier tanks. Passenger services were withdrawn in September 1938, but the line was taken over by the Royal Navy during World War II. As GWR No 28 Cleobury spent its last year in 1953 shunting at Dock Street, Newport.

Above: One of the least known and shortest-lived lines in Britain was the Edge Hill Light Railway, which opened in 1920 to serve some ironstone quarries in this part of the South Midlands and folded up when mining ceased five years later. Less than four miles in length, it was joined to the Stratford-upon-Avon & Midland Junction Railway at Burton Dassett, and operated in two separate sections linked by a rope-worked incline. The two locomotives used at the Burton Dassett end were both Stroudley 'Terriers' from the original batch of six built at Brighton in 1872. In this view No 1 is parked at the foot of the incline at Edge Hill on 11 May 1923. When sold by the LBSCR in 1919 it was reboilered Class A1X 0-6-0T No 673. After closure both engines lay derelict here for more than 20 years before being broken up by a local scrap merchant.

Above right: Another 'Brighton' exile was SR Class E1R 0-6-2T No 2095, which stands at Torrington station on 9 September 1933, awaiting departure with a train for Halwill Junction. First built 50 years previously as one of Stroudley's LBSCR Class E1 0-6-0Ts, it was among 10 selected for conversion and rebuilding with radial tanks in 1927-29 for use in the West Country. Several were drafted to the North Devon & Cornwall Junction Light Railway which had only opened in 1925. This line linked Torrington to the Bude and Padstow branches of the SR at Halwill Junction. Although displaced from here by Ivatt Class 2 2-6-2Ts in 1953, they were found other work and hung on for a few more years.

Right: High up on Exmoor, on the 1ft 11½in gauge Lynton & Barnstaple Railway, the 3.15pm train from Barnstaple Town to Lynton has just left Parracombe Halt on 7 September 1933. The locomotive is the last of the Manning Wardle 2-6-2Ts, No 188 Lew, which was supplied to the railway as late as 1925. Until then its three predecessors, supported by an American built Baldwin 2-4-2T, had operated services since the line opened in 1898. Taken over by the SR at the Grouping, this delightful railway was most unhappily closed just two years after this picture was taken, and all its engines scrapped except for Lew which was sent to Brazil.

Above: Down Ocean Liner express from Waterloo to Southampton Docks approaches Maybury box on 10 September 1931, with SR 'King Arthur' class N15 4-6-0 No E748 Vivien in charge. Built at Eastleigh in 1922, it was among the initial series of 20 engines designed by Robert Urie for the LSWR which were introduced in 1918.

This batch was never regarded as quite the equal of the later Maunsell 'Arthurs', but in performance there was little evidence to justify it. This engine was one of 10 Urie 'Arthurs' loaned to Heaton depot for freight work in the north-east in 1942-43, at a time during the war when the LNER was desperately short of motive power.

Above: Plymouth, Devonport & South Western Junction Railway 0-6-0T No 3 A. S. Harris stands at the bay platform at Bere Alston with the 2.15pm mixed train for the Callington branch on 7 April 1919. This was the junction with the main line to Plymouth over which the LSWR had running powers until it absorbed this Colonel Stephens' railway in 1922. Although the line north of Bere Alston was closed in 1968, the branch remains open as far as Gunnislake. This unique little engine was designed and built by Hawthorn Leslie in 1907 specially for tackling the steep gradients and sharp curves of the branch when it opened in March 1908. It continued to be so employed until 1929, but was then transferred away for its remaining 20 years.

Right: SR Class T9 4-4-0 No 724 rounds the bend out of Okehampton to begin the northern ascent on to Dartmoor with the 9.50am Portsmouth to Plymouth express on 8 September 1923. One of Dugald Drummond's famous 'Greyhounds', it had recently received the Eastleigh pattern superheater, which immeasurably improved the performance of this fast, free-running design. This engine was included in the first batch of 30 supplied by Dubs & Co to the LSWR in 1899, and lasted until May 1959.

Above: SR Class D1 0-4-2T No B224 is impatient to leave Rye with the 6.10pm auto-train to Hastings on 29 August 1931. The 'D-Tanks', as they were known, were another of Stroudley's efficient and economic designs for the LBSCR, and many were still to be found at this time all over the SR system, most of them well over 50 years old. This engine had been constructed at Brighton in 1885, and is seen here as rebuilt with Marsh boiler and cast-iron chimney. It ended its days with some others at Bricklayers Arms in 1940 sandbagged up as a form of air raid shelter.

Below: The lightly loaded 11am express from Charing Cross to Dover emerges from Martello Tunnel at Folkestone Warren on 31 August 1931, behind SR Class L 4-4-0 No A778. It was at this exact spot that the serious landslip and subsidence had occurred in December 1915, which caused the line to be abandoned until after the war. Wainwright's last design, this engine was one of 10 supplied to the SECR in 1914 by the German firm, A. Borsig of Berlin. The superbly constructed parts were shipped over and assembled at Ashford Works, all of which not surprisingly created something of a stir at the time. Apart from the other 12 of the class built by Beyer Peacock in the same year, apparently no British firm could meet the urgent delivery date.

Top: The SR turbine-driven SS Maid of Orleans puts to sea from Folkestone Harbour for the 3.50pm cross-Channel sailing to Boulogne on 27 March 1932. It had been operating on this route since conversion from coal to oil burning in 1926, and remained so employed until 1939. Completed at the William Denny yard at Dumbarton early in 1918, it was commissioned that summer as a troopship on the Southampton-Le Havre route for the last months of World War I. Joining the SECR fleet at the end of the war, it proved to be the last of these popular two-funnel steamers built for the company. Serving once again as a troopship during the Normandy landings in 1944, it unluckily struck a mine and was sunk, mercifully whilst on its way back from France.

Above: Nord Super-Pacific 4-6-2 No 3.1206 is cautiously escorted past a waiting chauffeur-driven limousine on the quay at Boulogne Maritime on arrival with the 16.00 Pullman Car boat express from Paris on 28 May 1927. A de Gleyn four-cylinder compound from the first series of 40 Bréville engines built at the Blanc-Misseron Works in 1923-24, it was fitted with single dome and separate sandbox with slide valves for the low pressure and piston valves for the high pressure cylinders, and also carries ACFI feed water apparatus. Capable of being worked by various means of simple or compound expansion made them difficult to handle, and although many lasted up to 1962 Chapelon Pacifics which arrived after 1934 were usually preferred for the principal trains.

Above left: The 18.26 Boulogne Ville-Calais Ville local train crosses the viaduct over the river at Wimereux on 26 May 1927, hauled by Nord 4-6-0 No 3.624. There were 149 de Gleyn-du Bousquet four-cylinder compounds of this type built between 1908 and 1912. Designed as mixed traffic engines they frequently handled the heaviest and most important passenger trains. One of them, No 3.628, has been purchased for active preservation in Britain on the Nene Valley Railway.

Left: Shunting carriage stock at Laroche on 9 September 1929, is one of the ancient 'Bourbonnais' type 0-6-0s of the PLM No 3 B 84, which dates from 1874. No less than 1,057 of these ubiquitous, long-lived goods engines were built between 1854 and 1882, and for several decades they bore the brunt of the company's freight workings. They were originally cabless, but other features clearly apparent include the large dome, Salter safety valves and the remarkably short wheelbase with firebox situated well behind the rear pair of coupled wheels. One of their number has been preserved by the SNCF in the French Railway Museum at Mulhouse.

Above right: PLM 4-6-2 No 231D89 was relaxing on the shed at Laroche on the same day as the old 0-6-0 seen opposite, 9 September 1929. A total of 285 of these four-cylinder compound Pacifics were built between 1922 and 1925. They differed from the earlier 231C series introduced in 1912 by combining the high and low pressure cut off to the cylinders. All were rebuilt gradually over the period from 1934 to 1950 with the addition of Dabeg feed water heater and double chimney, and were redesignated as 231G series.

Above: Leaving Dover Harbour on the 12.55pm sailing to Calais on 6 September 1931, is the single funnel turbine-driven SS Isle of Thanet. Together with the SS Maid of Kent II, they were two identical new ships having oil-fired water tube boilers, built by William Denny in 1925 for the Folkestone and Dover squadron of the SR fleet. During World War II both were employed as hospital ships, and Isle of Thanet survived to return to its Channel packet duties for many more years. Maid of Kent II was less fortunate, being sunk in Dieppe Harbour in May 1940 when full of wounded. A similar, but rather more luxurious vessel, the SS Canterbury II, was added for the introduction of the 'Golden Arrow' service in 1929.

Above: Belgian State Railways Class 8 bis 4-6-0 No 4618 hurries past Sarsultram with the 13.59 express from Brussels to Herbesthal on 20 September 1930. This was one of 75 engines ordered in 1919 but not delivered until 1921-23 because of postwar material shortages, which were an enlarged superheated development of a de Glehn-du Bousquet four-cylinder compound design of 1905. All were rebuilt after 1934, but this was one of two engines that received high pressure cylinders and divided drive, becoming Class 7/3 No 7.018. It was destroyed by military action in World War II.

Below: Belgian Marine turbine-driven SS Prince Léopold makes its way out of Dover Harbour past the end of the Prince of Wales Pier, as it begins the 12.30pm cross-Channel sailing to Ostend on 6 September 1931. It had been built by John Cockerill and launched at Hoboken only the previous year. When Belgium surrendered in 1940 during World War II, it was taken over by the Royal Navy and used as an infantry landing ship. It was present at the ill-starred Dieppe raid of August 1942, and participated in the Normandy D-Day landings two years later. Alas, on 29 July 1944, it was torpedoed by the German U-Boat No U621, and sank at a spot midway between Southampton and Arramanches.

Above: Soon after the Grouping, before Gresley Pacifics had begun to multiply, the newly established LNER transferred all six of Robinson's four-cylinder 4-6-0s of GCR Class 9P to work on the former GN main line between King's Cross and Leeds. Built at Gorton in 1920 and still in Great Central livery, No 1166 Earl Haig blasts noisily up to Wood Green in charge of the down 4pm express on 21 July 1923. Not a great success, they were returned to the GC section in 1927 to spend their remaining 20 years working mostly from Neasden and Immingham sheds on secondary duties. In 1943 this engine was singled out by Thompson for comprehensive rebuilding to resemble a 6ft 9in version of his own recently introduced two-cylinder Class B1, an event which may have prolonged its life by another two years.

Below: Altogether there were nine different, numerically small classes of 4-6-0 introduced by Robinson on the GCR in his largely unsuccessful search for a satisfactory design of this type. In this view at Skegness LNER Class B8 No 5280 is waiting to leave with the 7.50pm return excursion train to Bulwell Common, Nottingham, on 3 June 1934. Turned out from Gorton in January 1915, it belonged to the 'Glenalmond' class of 11 5ft 7in inside cylinder engines which were essentially a mixed traffic version of the 6ft 9in 'Sam Fays' (LNER Class B2). Initially handling fast fish trains from Grimsby to Marylebone, all were later allocated to Annesley or Colwick for a variety of freight and excursion work. They were withdrawn during 1947-49.

Left: Under a snow-laden sky and in bitterly cold weather late in the afternoon of 11 November 1919, NER Class C 0-6-0 No 1819 has been stopped at signals outside the eastern end of Newcastle Central station whilst heading a special accident van train from Gateshead to Newburn. It was the penultimate engine of a class totalling 201 when turned out from Gateshead Works at the end of 1894. Introduced in 1886, this was T. W. Worsdell's standard goods design, more powerful but having much in common with his equally successful Class Y14 engines of 1883 for the GER. The last survivor was LNER Class J21 No 65033, withdrawn only in April 1962, but rather lucky to have been preserved.

Below: Prototype NER 2-4-0 No 1463 waits for signals at Britannia Junction before proceeding with the 1pm Hull to Scarborough train on 22 June 1920. It originated as the product of the Works Committee under Henry Tennant, which was urgently formed following the sudden resignation of Alexander McDonnell in 1884, and 10 engines apiece were constructed by Darlington and Gateshead Works in 1885. This locomotive took part in the Stockton & Darlington Railway Centenary Procession in 1925, and after withdrawal in 1927 was preserved in the old York Railway Museum.

Above: Fletcher NER Class 1440 2-4-0 No 1448 is ready to leave from the eastern end of Newcastle Central station with the 1.17pm express for Middlesbrough on 20 November 1919. From a class of 15 engines it was first built at Gateshead in 1878, but received a Worsdell standard steel boiler in 1891. The design was similar to the earlier and better known Class 901, but with smaller 6ft coupled wheels. Only nine survived the Grouping and all disappeared very soon thereafter, this engine being withdrawn from Sunderland shed in August 1923.

Below: Raven NER mixed traffic Class S2 4-6-0 No 825 has been taking water in the yard at Heaton shed on 14 May 1920. The last engine of its class, it was built at Darlington in 1913 fitted with Stumpf uniflow cylinders, an experimental system of steam distribution. Later the last of the superheated three-cylinder Class Z Atlantics was similarly equipped, but there seemed little measurable benefit and No 825 was converted to standard in 1924 as LNER Class B15. Overshadowed by Raven's own superior three-cylinder engines of Class S3 (LNER Class B16) introduced at the end of 1919, all 20 of the earlier type had succumbed before Nationalisation in 1948.

Above: Beyond Montrose the NBR route to Aberdeen swung inland to join the Caledonian at Kinnaber Junction before returning to the sea at Stonehaven, whilst the 12-mile branch to Inverbervie continued north along the coast. LNER Class G9 0-4-4T No 9475 shuts off on approaching St Cyrus with the 4.57pm branch train from Montrose on 18 April 1930. A Reid NBR design for just this kind of work, it was the last in a total of 12 engines all built at the Hyde Park Works of the NBL Company 1909. It was also the last to be withdrawn in November 1940.

Below: An up Scottish express meat train draws out of Craigentinny yard on the evening of 21 August 1928, double-headed by LNER Class D34 4-4-0 No 9270 Glen Garry and Class K2 2-6-0 No 4701. These engines were almost exact contemporaries, being built respectively at Cowlairs in 1919 and by Kitson & Co at Leeds in 1921, and both belonged to classes used extensively on the West Highland line. The 'Glens' were the final, superheated development of 4-4-0 passenger locomotive designed by Reid for the NBR and introduced in 1913. On the other hand Gresley's 'Ragtimers', so called because of their reputation for rough riding, stemmed from one of his earliest designs for the GNR in 1912. This engine was among those of the class allocated to Scotland which later received a side-window cab and was named Loch Laggan.

Above: A brace of Caledonian Railway 'Dunalastairs' raise the echoes as they pass Tunnel box in a spectacular exit from Glasgow Buchanan Street double-heading the 10.17am special Pullman Car express to Oban on 5 August 1922. Coupled inside is 'Dunalastair II' class 4-4-0 No 779 Breadalbane *built in 1898, whilst the pilot engine is the slightly larger 'Dunalastair III' class 4-4-0 No 891 of 1900. Both were constructed at St Rollox and neither engine was ever superheated. At this time they were shedded at Callander and Balornock respectively, and both were eventually scrapped in 1939.*

Right: Two LNER Class D40 4-4-0s No 6852 Glen Grant *and* No 6854 Southesk *wait in Aberdeen station on 27 August 1927, for the arrival of the Royal Train from Euston conveying King George V and Queen Mary for the start of their summer holiday at Balmoral. They will take over the train for the 43-mile journey up the beautiful Deeside line to Ballater. Both these former GNSR locomotives, built by the NBL Company in 1920, were Heywood superheated versions of a Pickersgill design introduced in 1899. Altogether there were eight of these later engines, including* No 49 Gordon Highlander *now preserved in the Glasgow Museum of Transport.*

Below: Running tender first, LMS Class 3F 0-6-0 No 17562 eases its way cautiously down towards Oban with an officers' special from Glasgow in June 1925. One of McIntosh's large-boilered standard goods engines of the Caledonian 812 class, it was among the first batch of 17 built at St Rollox in 1899 which were fitted with Westinghouse brake for mixed traffic duties. The front two coaches were both designed as family saloons, the first being Caledonian six-wheeler No 1 followed by a Park LNWR bogie sleeping car of 1898.

Bottom: The midday train from Oban to Glasgow Buchanan Street on 13 April 1925, hauled by LMS Class 4P 4-6-0 No 14606 has just arrived at Connel Ferry, where it will pick up passengers from the Ballachulish branch. This engine belonged to the second generation of 'Oban Bogies' which formed the Caledonian 55 class. Five were built at St Rollox in 1902, plus a further four including this one in 1905. Designed by J. F. McIntosh, they were the first British inside-cylinder 4-6-0, and were notable for their small 5ft coupled wheels and exceptionally short wheelbase of only 11ft 3in. It made them ideally suited to this steeply-graded line, and No 14606 had become the last survivor when withdrawn from Oban in November 1937.

Above: Night time in Glasgow Central station sees brand new Caledonian Railway 72 class 4-4-0 No 78 waiting to leave with the 10.20pm sleeping car express for London Euston on 15 October 1920. It was only six weeks out of St Rollox Works and had been allocated to Carstairs shed. Designed by William Pickersgill and first introduced in 1916, these engines marked the final development of McIntosh's celebrated 'Dunalastairs'. Although not rated as powerful or free-running as the superheated 'Dunalastair IV' class, all 48 survived until 1959-62 except for one destroyed in the Gollanfield accident of 1953.

Below: Caledonian Railway 'River' class 4-6-0 No 940 storms past St Rollox as it gets the 7pm express goods for Carlisle under way on 4 August 1922. This was one of six locomotives designed by F. G. Smith and built by Hawthorn Leslie in 1915 for the Highland Railway. Incredibly at a time of desperate motive power shortage they were alleged to be too heavy for the Perth-Inverness main line, although they were later to work over it satisfactorily enough in LMS days. Sold direct to the Caledonian, they were reckoned the best 4-6-0s that company ever owned. Sent with one other survivor to end their days working Dalmellington-Ayr coal trains, where they were known locally as 'Scharnhorst' and 'Gneisenau', this engine expired spectacularly with a fractured cylinder whilst on one of these jobs in 1945.

Right: On the Highland main line near Dunkeld on 9 July 1932, the 3.40pm restaurant car express from Perth to Inverness approaches cautiously through the sylvan surroundings behind LMS Class 4P 4-6-0 No 14769 Clan Cameron. This was the last of the eight powerful 'Clan' class locomotives delivered to the Highland Railway by Hawthorn Leslie in 1919 and 1921. Designed by Smith's successor, Christopher Cumming, they provided the eventual solution to the passenger motive power problem on the main line after the 'River' class fiasco in 1915.

Below: By the shores of the Dornoch Firth on a September afternoon in 1923, the first of Peter Drummond's 'Barney' class 0-6-0s, No 134, makes a spirited departure from Tain with what by this point had become a fairly sizeable pick-up goods from Wick to Inverness. It had been built by Dubs & Co in 1900, and although shortly after the Grouping still retains its Highland livery and number. They were the only 0-6-0 tender engines the Highland Railway ever owned, and all but one survived until after World War II.

Left: An officers' special sets out from Inverness in September 1923 heading for Brora, more than half way to Wick, hauled by 'Loch' class 4-4-0 No 131 Loch Shin still sporting its Highland Railway colours. A total of 15 such locomotives was built by Dubs & Co in 1896. They were David Jones' last major design before the terrible accident that presaged his premature retirement. So dependable were they that 20 years after their first introduction three more of the class were ordered from Dubs' successor, the NBL Co, to meet the demands of additional wartime traffic on the Kyle line.

Below: Several of Stanier's ubiquitous LMS Class 5P5F 4-6-0s were sent new in 1935 to relieve ageing Highland locomotives in the far north of Scotland. Only a few months after delivery from Crewe Works, No 5003 approaches the junction with the Lybster branch on leaving Wick with the 10am 'John o'Groat' restaurant car express to Inverness on 23 August that year. It was among the second series of 20 'Black Fives' that followed the successful introduction the previous year of the first 50 built by the Vulcan Foundry. The class eventually reached the huge total of 842 engines, all of which lasted until the final years of steam in the 1960s and several have been preserved.

Left: A heavy train of empty coal wagons on the Llanelly & Mynydd Mawr Railway ascends the incline leading away from Llanelly on its return to the Great Mountain Colliery at Cross Hands some 12 miles inland on 13 May 1919. It is headed by Hudswell Clarke 0-6-0T Merkland, *built in 1912, and banked in the rear by Andrew Barclay 0-6-0T* George Waddell. *Opened in 1883, this freight only line was one of many small railways absorbed into the GWR system on 1 January 1923, and its eight locomotives were all taken into stock.* Merkland *was allocated No 937, but it was cut up at Swindon just four months later.*

Below: In the first year of amalgamation with the GWR, former Taff Vale Railway Class K 0-6-0 No 359, now carrying its allotted GWR No 1001, brings a heavy coal train down from Treherbert at the head of the Rhondda Valley in June 1922. Running tender first as was customary in this direction, it passes Radyr on its way to Penarth Docks. When built by Kitson & Company in 1885 it was almost the last of a large class of 85 engines, designed by Hurry Riches and introduced in 1874. It was also one of the last survivors when withdrawn at the end of 1926.

Left: On the Brecon & Merthyr Railway shortly before it was absorbed by the GWR in July 1922, the driver of 0-6-0ST No 8 is busy lubricating key points on his engine during a break in shunting at Merthyr. The goods depot of the adjoining Taff Vale Railway can be seen in the background. This locomotive was one of 12 built by Robert Stephenson in 1884 which were used mainly for mineral traffic, and it was stationed up at Brecon at this time. Becoming GWR No 2184, it was sent to Swindon the following October and rebuilt with 'Metro' type Belpaire boiler and pannier tanks. Subsequently based at Oswestry, it was scrapped in 1933.

Below: Cardiff Railway 0-6-0T No 7 belonged to the smallest of the constituent companies amalgamated with the GWR in 1922, but before that it is seen bustling away from Heath Halt with the 2.30pm railmotor train from Cardiff to Rhydyfelin on 17 May 1919. This was a brand new locomotive built by Kitson & Co earlier the same year, although the design was based on six engines supplied as much as 20 to 30 years previously. It had sloping side tanks to assist the driver's forward view, whilst on top it could accommodate up to 2 tons of coal. It became GWR No 685, and was sold to Carlton Main Colliery, Grimethorpe in 1931 where it lasted until 1953.

Left: Fresh from its triumphs in the historic locomotive exchange with the LNER in April and May of the same year, Collett four-cylinder 'Castle' class 4-6-0 No 4079 Pendennis Castle *takes the GWR stand at the British Empire Exhibition at Wembley on 10 October 1925. Looking quite resplendent, it gives no appearance of ever having been used. At the time only 20 engines of this famous class had been placed in service, but construction was to continue almost uninterrupted until 1950 when the total had reached 171, all built at Swindon. Withdrawal of these engines was completed in 1965, but several have been preserved, including No 4079 which has been shipped to Western Australia.*

Above left: Dean GWR double-framed 'Bulldog' class 4-4-0 No 3348 Launceston *has just arrived at Penzance with the midnight express from Paddington on 11 March 1919. Originating from Swindon in October 1900 in the series constructed with straight frames, it had been rebuilt in May 1911 with a superheated, long-coned boiler, and had also exchanged slide valves for piston valves in 1916. It has the oval-patterned combined name and number plates on the cab sides, but lost its name in 1930 along with others named after places as apparently passengers were mistaking them for train destinations. It was scrapped in 1934.*

Above: About to leave Newquay on 1 July 1921, with the 5pm train across Cornwall to connect with the main line at Par is GWR 4500 class 2-6-2T No 4510, a type familiar for so long on the branch lines of the south-west. One of Churchward's highly successful standard designs, with larger coupled wheels than the preceding 4400 class, there were 175 engines in all. No 4510 was built in 1907 among the original batch of 20 which turned out to be the last locomotives constructed at the Company's Wolverhampton Works. Several examples remain in service today on privately preserved railways.

Top: Metropolitan Railway Class G 0-6-4T No 97 Brill simmers quietly in the sunshine at Neasden shed on 7 August 1926. Designed by Charles Jones, it was the last of four engines supplied by the Yorkshire Engine Co in 1915-16. Forerunners of his efficient passenger Class H 4-4-4Ts, they were useful on any kind of work that the system required. Subsequently they were rather overshadowed by the big Class K 2-6-4Ts introduced in 1925, but along with both these other types they were sold to the LNER in 1937 and reclassified M2. As a non-standard class they would have been scrapped earlier but for the outbreak of World War II.

Above: The last of Charles Jones' passenger tank engines of Class H referred to previously, 4-4-4T No 110, sets off down hill from Chalfont & Latimer with the 5.4pm Chesham to Baker Street train on 10 June 1933. Eight of these engines were built for the Metropolitan Railway by Kerr Stuart in 1920-21 for working over the non-electrified lines north of Harrow and, after 1925, Rickmansworth. On entering LNER stock in 1937 they became Class H2 and were renumbered. At the end of 1941 all were transferred away to the Nottingham area based on Colwick, where they were not especially popular. They were gradually scrapped over the period 1942-47.

Above: On the exact day of the Centenary of the opening of the Liverpool & Manchester Railway on 15 September 1830, during a week of celebrations to mark this notable event, a special train was run from Liverpool to Manchester. Leaving at 11.40am it conveyed the Lord Mayor of Liverpool and civic representatives for the purpose of unveiling a commemorative tablet at the original railway station in Liverpool Road, Manchester, followed by a luncheon in the Town Hall. The train is seen approaching Huyton hauled by LMS 'Prince of Wales' class 4-6-0 No 5712, suitably decorated for the occasion. Not a particularly glamorous choice, this Bowen-Cooke LNWR locomotive had been built at Crewe in 1919 and was scrapped only 18 years later, a member of a large class that became obsolete very early.

Below: Although a replica of the famous Rocket took part in the Centenary celebrations, the oldest original engine of the Liverpool & Manchester Railway to be present was the veteran 0-4-2 No 57 Lion, which had been built by Todd, Kitson and Laird in 1838. It is seen here on Monday 15 September 1930, hauling a replica train of original stock and passengers in contemporary attire on the special track set up in the Exhibition grounds at Wavertree Park. After being withdrawn from normal service in 1859, it was subsequently used as a stationary boiler by the Mersey Docks and Harbour Board until purchased by the LMSR for preservation in 1928.

Above: Raven LNER Pacific Class A2/1 4-6-2 No 2401 City of Kingston upon Hull *ascends Cockburnspath bank with the up 'Queen of Scots' Pullman Car express in August 1932. It was the second of two engines of this NER design that were hastily completed at Darlington to beat the Grouping deadline on 1 January 1923. Three more of the class entered traffic in 1924, but with the outstanding success of Gresley's Pacifics it was understandable that they never really stood a chance. Working from Gateshead they were mostly confined to the East Coast main line, but were seldom seen in London until transferred to York in 1934. The need for new boilers and the arrival of Class V2 2-6-2s in 1936 sealed their fate, and all had been withdrawn by the following year.*

Below: Gresley LNER experimental high pressure four-cylinder compound Class W1 4-6-4 No 10000 pulls out of Darlington with a Leeds to Edinburgh express in June 1930. It was fitted with a Yarrow marine-type water tube boiler having a working pressure of 450lb/sq in. The secrecy surrounding its construction coupled with its singular appearance earned it the nickname 'Hush Hush' when it emerged from Darlington Works at the end of 1929. However, maintenance proved troublesome, and in 1937 Gresley converted it to a three-cylinder simple resembling his streamlined Class A4s. Although never their equal, its new dimensions made it the most powerful express passenger steam locomotive in Britain. It was withdrawn in 1960.

Top: The second of Gresley's big eight-coupled express passenger engines for the LNER pulls out of Kings Cross with the heavy 4pm train to Newcastle on 18 May 1935. The three-cylinder Mikado class P2/2 2-8-2 No 2002 Earl Marischal *had emerged from Doncaster Works in October 1934, and differed from the first engine,* Cock o' the North, *in having piston valves, the standard Gresley derived gear and an exhaust steam injector. As seen here it has been fitted with additional deflectors around the Kylchap double chimney to counter drifting steam from its soft exhaust. Both engines were later altered to conform with the four streamlined examples which followed in 1936, and the whole class was rebuilt by Thompson in 1943-44 as unstreamlined Pacifics forming Class A2/2.*

Above: LNER Class A1 4-6-2 No 4475 Flying Fox *has been slowed for signals as it runs cautiously through Durham station with the down 'Flying Scotsman' in July 1930. One of the first Gresley Pacifics, it was completed at Doncaster in April 1923 and sent straight to Top Shed where it was based until after the start of World War II. In March 1947 it was one of the last to receive the higher pressure boiler on conversion to Class A3. Shortly before withdrawal at the end of 1964, the veteran engine was chosen for a special last run from Kings Cross to Doncaster on 2 May that year, long after steam had been banished from the London end of the East Coast main line.*

Opposite page: LNER Class A4 4-6-2 No 2509 Silver Link has been slowed almost to a standstill by adverse signals as it passes through Wood Green station several minutes ahead of schedule. It has reached the last lap of its four hour dash to London with the up 'Silver Jubilee' express from Newcastle on 3 May 1937. At this time steam traction was at the zenith of its considerable achievements, and nowhere was this more thrillingly demonstrated than with Sir Nigel Gresley's high speed streamlined fliers of the East Coast main line. Although six members of this celebrated class have been preserved, Silver Link is regrettably not among them.

Above: One of Gresley's best locomotive designs for the LNER was the mixed traffic three-cylinder Class V2 2-6-2 introduced in 1936. Romping past Cherry Burton in fine style on 19 October 1937, at the head of the ubiquitous LNWR Royal Train returning from Hull to York is No 4780 The Snapper, The East Yorkshire Regiment, The Duke of York's Own. It had been completed at Darlington just the previous August, and officially named at Hull Paragon station the following month. In a large class of 184 engines only eight were destined to receive names. The prototype No 4771 Green Arrow happily continues to play an active role on the preservation scene.

Above: LNER Class C2 4-4-2 No 3250 leaves Potters Bar with the 2.30pm stopping train from Kings Cross to Hitchin on 27 September 1935. This was the day of the historic trial trip of the 'Silver Jubilee' which had left London just five minutes earlier than this train, but no onlookers have stayed to witness the veteran Ivatt Atlantic go by. The GNR prototype, No 990 Henry Oakley, had been the first of its type in Britain on appearing from Doncaster Works in 1898. For no better reason than that their introduction coincided with American Gold Rush fever these small-boilered Atlantics were nicknamed 'Klondykes'. No more were built for two years, and eventually the class was limited to 22 engines, for they were soon overshadowed by the famous large-boilered version that followed in 1902.

Below: LNER Class B12 4-6-0 No 8537 passes Goodmayes on 28 September 1937, with the 12.53pm Liverpool Street-Ipswich stock train, a description that just about covers the miscellaneous collection of vehicles that made up this working. Built at Stratford in 1915, this engine belonged to the GER's last express passenger class which had been designed by S. D. Holden. In 1932 it was fitted with ACFI feed water heating apparatus, carried for a time by most of the class, earning for them the nickname 'Camels' or 'Hikers' if serving in Scotland. This was removed in 1939 when the engine was rebuilt by Gresley with larger boiler and round-topped firebox to Class B12/3. Withdrawal was in 1957.

Above: LNER Class 02 2-8-0 No 3461 nears Potters Bar at the head of a Peterborough to Ferme Park coal train on 14 June 1932. Built at Doncaster for the GNR in 1918, this was Gresley's first three-cylinder locomotive, experimentally incorporating Walschaerts valve gear with his own derived motion for the inside cylinder. It was an immediate success, but later engines not only had enlarged cylinders and increased boiler pressure but received the altered arrangement of conjugated valve gear that became standard. It was never brought into line, which must have hastened its comparatively early demise in 1948. The unusually large dome hides the top feed apparatus with which it has been fitted.

Below: Gresley LNER three-cylinder Class K3/2 2-6-0 No 135 storms up the last mile to Potters Bar with the 6pm ex-Belle Isle down Scottish express goods on 29 July 1931. These powerful Moguls with big 6ft diameter boilers were the first type to incorporate the standard Walschaerts valve gear and derived motion when introduced on the GNR at Doncaster in 1920. This engine was built at Darlington in 1925, and further examples continued to appear from various sources up to 1937, when the class totalled 193. All were withdrawn between 1959 and 1962.

Above: Near Hatch End on 21 March, 1936, LMS Class 7F (later 8F) 2-8-0 No 8006 double-head a down empty coal train from Stonebridge Park which includes 10 40ton bogie hopper wagons. The leading engine came from Bowen-the large family of LNWR freight locomotives of this type, and was one of Bowen-Cooke's superheated two-cylinder simples of Class G1 which had been rebuilt in 1921 from a Webb four-cylinder compound of 1901. Coupled inside was one of Stanier's classic heavy freight locomotives, of which only the first 12, initially fitted with domeless taper boilers, had been placed in service at this date. Receding in the opposite direction is an LPTB Bakerloo Line tube train, which were not then confined to peak journeys to Watford Junction.

Right: After the Grouping until World War II a regular LMS intrusion on to the East Coast main line of the LNER could be seen in the suburban workings from Broad Street that dated back to a concession won by the North London Railway from the GNR in 1875. Hence Stanier Class 3P 2-6-2T No 105 climbs away from New Barnet with the 5.12pm Broad Street to Potters Bar local train on 3 June 1938. This engine had been built at Derby in 1935 with domeless taper boiler and top feed, and although the class totalled 139 their reputation for poor steaming rated them the least successful of the great engineer's designs.

Below: LMS 'Precursor' class 4-4-0 No 5304 Greyhound approaches Headstone Lane on the up slow line in charge of the 4.30pm local train from Bletchley to Euston on 29 June 1935. There was a total of 130 of these express passenger engines designed by George Whale for the LNWR in 1904, but their importance had already declined before the Grouping. This one had emerged from Crewe in July 1905, and by 1922 had been rebuilt with superheated Belpaire boiler and piston valves. It had eventually become the penultimate survivor when condemned at the beginning of 1947.

Above: Stanier's third LMS Pacific, the experimental turbine-driven Class 7P 4-6-2 No 6202, gathers speed past Brent Junction box with the 10.40am Euston to Liverpool express, 'The Manxman', on 11 September 1935. Less than three months out of Crewe Works, it was still fitted with the initial 32-element superheater and domeless boiler. For much of its existence the 'Turbomotive', as it was known, was employed on the 8.30am down 'Merseyside Express' and 5.25pm return. Indeed it was on this schedule when destroyed in the Harrow & Wealdstone accident of October 1952, only a few weeks after conversion to a conventional four-cylinder engine, which differed in several respects from the 'Princess Royal' class.

Left: Fowler LMS three-cylinder 'Royal Scot' class 4-6-0 No 6152 The King's Dragoon Guardsman picks up water at speed on Dillicar troughs in the Lune Valley south of Tebay as it heads north with the 9.27am Crewe-Perth express on 24 August 1939. It has always been believed that this engine was the original No 6100 after it had exchanged names and numbers with the Derby-built No 6152 for the tour of the USA and Canada in 1933. From 1943 the whole class was most successfully rebuilt by Stanier with taper boilers and new cylinders, which saw them through to the early 1960s.

Above: LMSR up 'Coronation Scot' express catches the late evening sunlight as it hurries past Kenton on the last lap into Euston on 13 July 1937. Leaving Glasgow at 1.30pm it was allowed $6\frac{1}{2}$ hours for the 401.4-mile journey with a single stop at Carlisle. The service had been inaugurated the previous week, when only three of Stanier's new streamlined 'Coronation' class 4-6-2s had been completed although two more arrived very shortly. This is No 6222 Queen Mary resplendent in blue and silver livery. In spite of their impressive appearance the streamlined casing was not as effective as on the Gresley counterparts, and the locomotives were actually improved when this was removed after World War II.

Below: Another LMS 'Royal Scot' class 4-6-0 No 6130 Liverpool approaches Berkhamsted beside the Grand Union Canal heading the 11.30am Euston-Glasgow express on 20 August 1933. The first 50 of these Fowler engines were constructed with great urgency in two batches of 25 simultaneously in 1927 by the NBL Co in its two Glasgow works. No 6130 was turned out from the former Neilson Reid works at Hyde Park in August of that year, and received the name of an old Liverpool & Manchester Railway engine. This was changed in 1936 to The West Yorkshire Regiment when it was decided to adopt military style names for the whole class. Rebuilding with Stanier taper boiler was carried out at the end of 1949.

Above: GWR 'King' class 4-6-0 No 6009 King Charles II *stands alongside the coaling stage at Old Oak Common shed on 19 October, 1935. Introduced by Collett in 1927 to meet the heaviest traffic demands, all 30 of these large four-cylinder engines had been completed at Swindon by 1930. They proved to be the most powerful of their type in Britain with a phenomenal tractive effort of 40,300lb. Coupled wheels of 6ft 6in were slightly smaller than those of a 'Castle', but the axle load was increased to 22½tons which imposed severe route availability restrictions. The rapid spread of Western Region dieselisation by 1962 saw 21 of the class condemned with undignified haste that year, and the remainder were soon to follow.*

Below: Near the same spot at Old Oak Common some three years earlier on 24 September 1932, 'Castle' class 4-6-0 No 4000 North Star *replenishes its tender before backing down to Paddington to take out a Bristol express. Bearer in turn of perhaps the most celebrated name on the GWR, this engine's story had begun back in 1906 when Churchward produced at Swindon a high pressure four-cylinder simple 4-4-2 No 40 for direct comparison with the three de Glehn compound Atlantics recently purchased from France. From this emerged in the following year the first of his famous 'Star' class 4-6-0s, to which No 40 was shortly converted in 1909. It became No 4000 in 1912, and then in 1929 was the last of five 'Stars' to be rebuilt as 'Castle' class locomotives. In this ultimate state it survived until May 1957.*

Above: Another GWR 'Castle' class locomotive suffered the indignity of a partial streamlining experiment in March 1935, along with 'King' class 4-6-0 No 6014 King Henry VII. *Interestingly this operation preceded by six months the appearance of Gresley's first streamlined Pacific. The engine affected was No 5005* Manorbier Castle, *seen here heading west past Dawley Box with the 10.55am Saturdays only express from Paddington to Torquay and Paignton on 31 August 1935. Coverings over the outside cylinders, outside steampipes and front steam chests were removed very soon after this photograph was taken, but full restoration was not completed for more than another 10 years.*

Below: The 7.45am Fridays only through express from Penzance to Birmingham on 28 August 1936, was a light task for Churchward GWR four-cylinder 'Star' class 4-6-0 No 4019 Knight Templar, *as it runs beside the seawall near Teignmouth. This engine was among the second batch of 'Stars' built at Swindon in 1908. The 61 members of the class in service before World War I could fairly be said to represent the peak of express passenger locomotive development up to that time. Although gradually displaced by the larger 4-6-0s in later years, they always remained most reliable performers with several survivors lasting until the early 1950s.*

Above: Maunsell SR 'Schools' class 4-4-0 No 937 Epsom *is at Nine Elms shed on 11 June 1939, whilst running in after overhaul at Eastleigh Works and before returning to Bricklayers Arms, where it was stationed for most of its working life. It has just been fitted with Lemaître blastpipe and large diameter plain stovepipe chimney, and also extended smokebox to accommodate new Bulleid cylinders. There were 40 of these extremely capable three-cylinder engines built at Eastleigh between 1930 and 1935, and they proved to be the last 4-4-0s to appear in Britain. Much of their best work was done on the Hastings line for which their cabs were designed to suit the restrictive loading gauge.*

Below: 'Lord Nelson' class 4-6-0 No E864 Sir Martin Frobisher *makes a handsome sight on the down 'Golden Arrow' as it heads the Paris bound express near Bickley Junction on Sunday, 29 June 1930. In the decade before World War II this most prestigious of all the Southern Railway's trains was almost invariably in the hands of one of these big four-cylinder Maunsell locomotives. Primarily designed to meet the growing demand for adequate power on the heavy Continental boat expresses from Victoria to Dover and Folkestone, the prototype No E850* Lord Nelson *had appeared in 1926 and a further 15 were built at Eastleigh during 1928-29. After the war they became almost exclusively identified with the Bournemouth line services until their withdrawal was completed in 1962.*

Above: Moving into the era after World War II sees Bulleid 'Battle of Britain' class 4-6-2 No 21C162 storming through West Dulwich station in charge of the 9.20am Victoria-Dover Marine Continental Pullman Car express on 25 July 1948. Turned out at Brighton Works in May 1947, it is still in SR malachite green livery, and has not yet received its allocated name of 17 Squadron *or modified V-fronted cab. Identical with the 'West Country' class first introduced in 1945, these three-cylinder light Pacifics had much the same features as the earlier 'Merchant Navy' class, but a reduced weight which allowed almost maximum route availability. The final total of 110 engines seemed rather more than the system demanded and was extravagant motive power for many of the allotted duties.*

Above: The first of all the Bulleid Pacfics, SR 'Merchant Navy' class 4-6-2 No 21C1 Channel Packet, resplendent in malachite green livery, surges towards Bickley Junction box heading for Dover in charge of the down postwar 'Golden Arrow' all Pullman Car express on Friday, 19 April 1946. This famous train had been revived only on the previous Monday, prior to which the locomotive had visited Eastleigh to be prepared and fitted out with arrows and headboard, but it remained on the service for only a short time before returning to the Western Section. Since first emerging from Eastleigh Works in June 1941, it had undergone several modifications, and as seen here has short smoke deflector plates and still retains original cylinder casing.

Below: SR Class Q1 0-6-0 No C37 passes Maybury on the down slow line with a Nine Elms-Woking goods train on 12 May 1947. For working freight services with the widest possible route availability, Bulleid had designed a powerful locomotive, restricted to a weight of 52ton, but with a large boiler having a working pressure of 230lb and a heating surface in the firebox of 170sq ft. It resulted in the appearance of perhaps the most austere and ugly steam locomotive ever seen in Britain. Shared between Brighton and Ashford Works, 40 of these engines were built at the height of the war during 1942. They proved to be the last development of the 0-6-0 goods type so universally employed throughout the country for the previous 100 years.

*Right: On the same day Maunsell SR
'Schools' class 4-4-0 No 30924 Haileybury
gets away smartly from Sandling Junction
with the lightly loaded 11.20am express
from Folkestone Junction to Charing
Cross. Completed at Eastleigh in
December 1933, this engine saw service
successively on the Portsmouth Harbour
and Bournemouth routes until transferred
to Dover at the end of 1945. It received its
multiple jet blastpipe and large diameter
chimney in September 1940. Withdrawal
of the whole class of 40 engines was
concentrated in the period 1961-62.*

*Below: Neatly framed by the over-bridge at
the London end of Sandling Junction
station, new Bulleid SR 'Battle of Britain'
class 4-6-2 No 34088 213* Squadron *pulls
in with the 11.15am Charing Cross-
Margate via Dover express on 2
September 1949. It was among the first
batch of 20 built at Brighton after
Nationalisation, and entered traffic at the
end of 1948 allocated at Ramsgate shed.
The locomotive weight had been
marginally increased, and the group were
the first to be fitted with the larger
5,500gal tender. After 1956 all the
'Merchant Navy' class and over half the
light Pacifics were rebuilt with
Walschaerts valve gear and the air-
smoothed casing removed. This engine was
so dealt with in April 1960 and was
withdrawn in March 1967.*

Above: SR Class J1 4-6-2T No 2325 enters South Croydon station at the head of the 8.2pm Victoria-Tunbridge Wells West stopping train on 7 August 1947. Designed by Marsh as perhaps the most suitable type for operating the LBSCR's relatively short distance main line expresses, it was completed at Brighton at the end of 1910. After comparative fuel consumption trials with other classes, a second Pacific tank was built in 1912 incorporating Walschaerts in place of Stephenson valve gear and other modifications by L. B. Billinton, and classified J2. They were named Abergavenny and Bessborough respectively until 1924-25. Both were a familiar sight on this train in the years immediately following World War II while based at Tunbridge Wells West, but they were eventually displaced by new Fairburn LMS 2-6-4Ts and condemned in June 1951.

Below: SR Class L1 4-4-0 No 31759 completes a picturesque scene at Rye as it crosses the old Royal Military Canal approaching the station with the 11.55am Ashford-Hastings train on 7 May 1955. A total of 15 of these engines were hurriedly built by the NBL Co in 1926, primarily to meet the increasing demands of the Folkestone express services. They were a post-Grouping development by Maunsell with increased boiler pressure and smaller cylinders of Wainwright's SECR Class L of 1914. Always capable performers, they were still handling some Kent Coast expresses until electrification was completed in 1959, but their demise soon followed.

Above: *LNER Class A1 4-6-2 No 4470* Great Northern *stands in Belle Isle yard outside Kings Cross on 5 October 1946. Three days later it was renumbered 113. Many people were horrified when in 1945 the premier Gresley Pacific of 1922 was selected by Thompson for a comprehensive rebuild. After the style of his various Class A2s, this included conversion to three separate sets of Walschaerts valve gear with 10in piston valves, placing the outside cylinders to the rear of the bogie and fitting Kylchap double blastpipe and chimney. The large smoke deflectors were added not long afterwards. No other Gresley Pacific was affected in this way, and construction of new Class A1s based on this prototype was deferred until after Peppercorn had taken office. The engine remained in service until November 1962.*

Below: *Thompson LNER Class A2/1 4-6-2 No 507 has been checked by signals outside Finsbury Park with the 1.50pm stopping train from Peterborough to Kings Cross on 2 September 1946. Entering traffic in 1944-45, the four 6ft 2in Pacifics that made up this class were developed from the Gresley Class V2 2-6-2s, and indeed replaced the last four of those engines on order from Darlington Works. At the front end features were similar to the rebuilt* Great Northern, *but the cab and tender were identical to the 'V2s'. However, on its first heavy repair at the end of 1945 this engine received the tender off the Class A4 No 4469 destroyed in the air raid on York in June 1942. Large smoke deflectors replaced the small chimney-bracket type in November 1946, and it was named* Highland Chieftain *in May 1947.*

Above: Peppercorn Class A1 4-6-2 No 60140 climbs Holloway bank with the 10.5am Kings Cross-Glasgow express on 1 July 1949. Although obviously of LNER lineage the 49 Pacifics of this class were all built after Nationalisation. The intention had always been to develop these 6ft 8in engines after the rebuilt No 4470 Great Northern of 1945, and whilst various schemes for their ultimate design had been worked out during Thompson's regime, eventual construction was authorised by his successor. This was one of the 23 Darlington-built engines completed at the end of 1948 and subsequently named Balmoral.

Below: In 1947, Thompson's successor, Peppercorn, quickly produced an improved version of his predecessor's 6ft 2in class A2 Pacifics, incorporating a shorter wheelbase and moving the outside cylinders back in line with the bogie, but reverting to a single chimney. As with the Thompson engines, which were reclassified A2/3, 15 examples were built, all at Doncaster. The first of these, suitably named after its designer, LNER three-cylinder Class A2 4-6-2 No 525 A. H. Peppercorn, waits for signals to clear at Belle Isle box before backing down to Kings Cross station to take out an express for Newcastle on 23 April 1948. The last survivors were withdrawn in 1966, but one of the class, No 532 Blue Peter, has been preserved.

Above: After World War II the LNER continued its practice of allocating locomotives specially for royal duties, and choice fell upon the first of the recent Class B17 4-6-0 rebuilds to Class B2, No 1671 Manchester City, which name was changed to Royal Sovereign. Here it is approaching Brookmans Park with the 5.15pm Royal Special from Cambridge to Kings Cross on 3 June 1947. The formation includes one of the two 1908 12-wheeled Royal Saloons, but the King himself would not have been travelling as the royal headcode is not carried. In pursuit of his standardisation proposals, Thompson rebuilt 10 of these 6ft 8in Gresley engines with two cylinders and 100A (B1 type) boiler at an increased working pressure of 225lb. All were withdrawn from service in 1958-59.

Above: Close to its 8pm departure time, LNER Class B1 4-6-0 No 1003 Gazelle *prepares to leave Liverpool Street for Parkeston Quay with the down 'Hook Continental' boat express on 15 May 1947. Included in the initial series of ten engines, it had emerged from Darlington Works in November 1943 as No 8304, and must have looked well here in its postwar apple green livery lined out in black and white. Increasing numbers of this class were providing a much needed boost to express traffic on the GE section at this time. The first and most successful of all Thompson's designs, they ultimately totalled 410 examples delivered over the period 1942-52, and lasted until the final decline of steam in the mid-1960s.*

Below: Although probably best remembered for his endless attempts at improving Gresley's locomotives, Edward Thompson introduced in 1945 the third of only four new designs. This was a two-cylinder 2-6-4T, a type virtually unknown on the LNER, but which had been pioneered with success by both Fowler and Stanier on the LMS before World War II. The prototype Class L1 No 9000 appears here in apple green livery on an outer suburban train at Chelmsford on 26 April 1947. Eventually 100 of these engines were built, only the first at Doncaster, and distributed to many parts of the former LNER system. Although prone to more than their reasonable share of mechanical upsets, they had good acceleration in spite of the small 5ft 2in coupled wheels, and proved very efficient on secondary passenger and fast suburban trains.

Above: Newcomer coasting down into Marylebone on arrival with a regular interval auto-train from West Ruislip on 15 July 1949, is LNER Class N7/2 0-6-2T No 69689. A post-Grouping development of Hill's highly successful GER suburban tanks of Class L77, this engine was included in a batch of 20 supplied by Beardmore & Co in 1927 fitted with Belpaire firebox, steam brake and vacuum ejector. Twelve were subsequently altered to the Westinghouse brake, but the remainder received vacuum-controlled push-and-pull gear from June 1949, and five were posted to Neasden to operate this short-lived service.

Below: LNER Class L1 2-6-4T No 67751 makes a vigorous start from the former GCR terminus at Marylebone with the 6.30pm suburban train to High Wycombe on 21 July 1949. The extensive trials of the prototype delayed delivery of the remainder of this class until after Nationalisation. This locomotive was included among an order for 35 built by the NBL Co, arriving new at Neasden in December 1948. Like all the later engines it was equipped with steam brakes after the first 39 had received the Westinghouse pattern. As with other new steam designs after World War II, these Thompson engines had very short working lives, and withdrawal was completed between 1960-62.

Above: Robinson LNER Class A5/1 4-6-2T No 9819, built by the GCR at Gorton in 1917, storms out of Marylebone with the 1.4pm special train to Wembly Stadium for the Rugby League Cup Final on 7 May 1949. It carries the special headcode used at that time by all trains travelling via the Stadium loop line. With a few intermittent exceptions all 31 engines of this class *were based at Neasden until their very last years, and during the inter-war period no London commuters were better served than those using the routes into this terminus. They proved so satisfactory that Gresley had 13 more (Class A5/2) built by Hawthorn Leslie in 1925-26 slightly modified for the north-eastern area.*

Above: New Ivatt LMS Class 2P 2-6-2T No 1207 prepares to leave Kentish Town shed on 21 May 1947. Boasting almost maximum route availability, these versatile light duty tank engines were soon to become familiar over much of the British Railways' system. The first 10 were built at Crewe before Nationalisation, but the class eventually totalled 130 by 1953, and 30 more were added in the BR standard design of the 84000 series. It appears that four have been preserved, and No 1241 from the Keighley & Worth Valley Railway was included in the Rail 150 cavalcade in 1975.

Above right: Double chimney Class 4 2-6-0 No 43001, one of 10 built at Horwich for the LMS just prior to Nationalisation, heads the 2.5pm Aylesbury-Bletchley goods past Mentmore Crossing on the branch from Cheddington on 17 June 1950. These mixed traffic locomotives, also by Ivatt, were designed to replace the numerous, ageing LMS 0-6-0 freight types, and a total of 162 had been constructed up to 1952. Originally the first

50 were fitted with double blastpipes and chimneys, but this arrangement proved unsatisfactory and was soon altered. A further 115 engines were built to the modified BR standard design in the 76000 series. The Severn Valley Railway now have No 43106 which also appeared in the Rail 150 cavalcade.

Right: Another of H. G. Ivatt's designs, Class 2 2-6-0 No 46465 pulls out of Colchester with the 5.30pm Clacton-Cambridge train on 5 August 1951. It was the first engine in a batch of 18 built at Darlington this same year, and was allocated new to Cambridge where it remained throughout the 1950s. They were an exact tender version of the Class 2 2-6-2T in the adjoining picture. The original 20 engines had been built for the LMS, but construction continued after Nationalisation until the class had reached a total of 128 by 1953. Another 65 were added in the slightly modified BR standard design of the 78000 series. Several of these locomotives survive in various states of preservation.

Top: Local morning goods train from Willesden Junction to Watford Junction makes cautious progress along the down slow line north of Hatch End on 3 August 1946, with LMS Class 2F 0-6-0 No 3603 in charge. This 5ft 3in engine stemmed from the large family of standard Midland goods locomotives introduced by Johnson in 1875, which allowing for variations had reached by 1908 the huge total of 976. Although at one time it had carried the larger Class 3 boiler, it has been rebuilt with small unsuperheated Belpaire boiler and Deeley cab. In this condition it lasted until 1960 as BR No 58295.

Above: Fowler LMS Class 3P 2-6-2T No 25 bustles away from Elstree with the 2.5pm St Pancras-St Albans local suburban train on Saturday 5 June 1948. There were 70 of these passenger tank engines built at Derby between 1930-32, several including No 25 being fitted with condensing apparatus for working through the tunnels to Moorgate. Interestingly they carried a superheated version of the Belpaire boiler used on the rebuilt Johnson 0-6-0 shown above, which did nothing to help a basically poor, under-boilered design. Nevertheless they gave about 30 years' service, and were not extinct until 1962.

Above: The 3.55pm auto-train from St Albans to Watford Junction arrives at Bricket Wood on 5 September 1947, propelled by LMS Class 1P 2-4-2T No 6725. These ideal branch line tank engines of the former 910 class were brought out by Webb for the LNWR in 1890, and a total of 160, which included 40 converted from the old 2-4-0 'Precursors', was built up to 1897. This engine was shortly to be withdrawn, and only 19 survived long enough to receive BR numbering. The last example was taken out of service in 1955.

Below: In the bay platform next to the up slow line at Leighton Buzzard on 17 June 1950, the 5.38pm branch train for Dunstable waits to leave behind LMS Class 2F 0-6-2T No 58926. This was one of the splendid Webb 'Coal Tanks' of the LNWR, of which 300 were built at Crewe between 1881 and 1896. Dating from 1888, it was reprieved from the scrap-heap by the outbreak of World War II, and had become the last survivor when withdrawn from Abergavenny in 1958. Subsequently restored to LNWR livery with its original No 1054, it was first preserved at Penrhyn Castle and has latterly been at the Dinting Railway Centre. In 1980 it took part in the Rocket 150 cavalcade at Rainhill.

Above: British double summer time made it possible for this photograph to be taken at 9.32pm on 27 June 1947, of the 8.40pm down 'Irish Mail' express from Euston approaching Tring at the summit of the long climb into the Chilterns. The sparkling locomotive is LMS rebuilt 'Royal Scot' class 4-6-0 No 6112 Sherwood Forester, *which had been one of the first to receive Stanier taper boiler, new cylinders and double chimney in September 1943. Smoke deflectors were not fitted until 1949. In company with No 6127* Old Contemptibles *it was stationed at Holyhead for several years around this time especially for 'Irish Mail' duty.*

Right: LMS 'Princess Coronation' class 4-6-2 No 46239 City of Chester *speeds towards Watford tunnel with the 10am down 'Royal Scot' from Euston to Glasgow on 6 September 1948. These celebrated Stanier Pacifics first began to appear in 1937 in distinctive streamlined form with striking red or blue livery. By the end of World War II there were 33 of the class in service, including nine which had been built without streamlining. The embellishment was found to hinder maintenance, and consequently removed from all those affected. Smoke deflectors were then added, but the sloping top to the smokebox as seen on No 46239 remained a feature of the de-streamlined engines for several more years. Their end came swiftly in a mass withdrawal of the class's survivors in September 1964.*

104

Above: Heading north past Elsenham with the 7.28am express goods from Temple Mills to Whitemoor on 14 July 1951, is 'Austerity' Class WD 2-8-0 No 90064. Designed by R. A. Riddles and introduced in 1943, large numbers of these Ministry of Supply heavy freight locomotives had been built by the NBL Co and the Vulcan Foundry during the war, and this engine was among 200 taken into LNER stock in 1946 as class 07. A further 533 were purchased by BR in 1948, many of them returning from wartime service in Europe. They provided much needed support all over the country during those difficult postwar years.

Above: The most comprehensive locomotive exchanges in British railway history took place in the early months following Nationalisation in 1948. On 20 May that year GWR 'King' class 4-6-0 No 6018 King Henry VI had been rostered for its official test run to the 1.10pm express from Kings Cross to Leeds and Bradford. Seen here leaving the London terminus with a full load of 525ton, this 1928-built engine was by several years the senior competitor, ahead of the rebuilt 'Royal Scot', the 'Princess Coronation', the 'Merchant Navy' and the Class A4. It made the cleanest start by passing Finsbury Park in 7min 11sec, but thereafter running was unexceptional and not to be compared with the performance of Pendennis Castle 23 years earlier, even though Leeds was reached two minutes ahead of schedule.

Above: Within a few days of completion at Swindon Works new 'Castle' class 4-6-0 No 7007 Ogmore Castle hurries towards Iver in charge of the 1.18pm express from Paddington to Bristol on 10 July, 1946. Fitted with three-row superheater and mechanical lubricator, it was the final engine in a batch of 10 delivered that year when further construction of this famous class was resumed under the Hawksworth regime immediately after the war. Although 30 more were to appear during 1948-50, it proved to be the last main line passenger locomotive to be built for the GWR. Thus on Nationalisation in January 1948 it was singularly appropriate that its name was changed to Great Western.

Below: Hawksworth GWR 'County' class 4-6-0 No 1013 approaches West Ealing as it coasts towards Paddington with the 9am express from Bristol and Weston-super Mare on 13 July 1946. Introduced the previous year, these powerful mixed traffic engines retained the basic two-cylinder design which marked their development from Churchward's 'Saint' class of 1902. New features included coupled wheels of 6ft 3in and Standard No 15 boiler with 280lb pressure, which produced an impressive tractive effort of 32,580lb. A total of 30 was built at Swindon within two years, but the first 19 did not immediately receive names and No 1013 became County of Dorset only in January 1947. They were not notably free-runners, and possessed of a heavy hammer-blow that ensured they were never favourites with the Civil Engineer's department. All were withdrawn in 1962-64 before the end of steam on the Western Region.

Above: SR Class A1X 0-6-0T No 2678 emerges from St Michaels Tunnel into the sunlight on the Kent & East Sussex Railway with the 12.30pm mixed train from Headcorn to Rolvenden on 16 September 1946. This Stroudley 'Terrier' had been on loan to the railway since April 1941 and indeed remained until 1958. It had first been built by the LBSCR at Brighton in 1880 as No 78 Knowle, and was reboilered to Class A1X in 1911. After a spell in the Isle of Wight it narrowly escaped scrapping at Eastleigh at the end of 1936, was repaired and returned to service on the Hayling Island branch. When finally withdrawn by BR from Newhaven in 1963 it was sold to Butlin's Holiday Camp at Minehead, and is at present on the West Somerset Railway.

Below: On 28 June 1958, the LCGB ran its 'North Western Branch Lines' railtour which included the enterprising idea of using Service Locomotive No CD7, one of three remaining former LNWR Class 2F 0-6-0STs still employed at Wolverhampton Carriage Works, for traversing the Newport Pagnell branch. Meanwhile the other two, No CD3 of 1880 and No CD6 of 1875, were positioned for the photographers at Wolverton station. These engines were the Webb version of Ramsbottom's 'Special tank', of which 258 were built at Crewe during the period 1870-80. The last survivor in the active list had gone a long time previously in 1941, and the present trio were to follow within a year of this event.

Above: LNER Class E4 2-4-0 No 62786 pulls strongly away from Long Melford Junction past the prematurely cancelled home starter with the 1.33pm Cambridge-Colchester train on 30 October 1954. Dating from 1895, this engine was one of James Holden's GER Class T26, known as 'Intermediates', of which 100 were turned out at Stratford between 1891 and 1902. Designed for just such cross-country branch work, it was among the final 18 that survived intact throughout the period 1940-54. The last of the class was No 62785, withdrawn at the end of 1959 and now restored to Great Eastern colours in the National Railway Museum.

Below: GWR 2-4-0 No 1336 relaxes in the sunshine in front of a 'Hall' class 4-6-0 on Reading shed without apparently much to do on Saturday 1 June 1946. It had formerly belonged to the Midland & South Western Junction Railway, but was taken over when that company was absorbed in July 1923. Three of these engines had been supplied by Dubs & Co in 1894, and all were rebuilt at Swindon with Standard No 11 boilers in 1924. For some years after that the trio were employed on the Lambourn Valley branch, but latterly they pottered around in the Reading and Didcot areas. They were the only M&SW engines to survive World War II, and No 1336 was last to go in 1954.

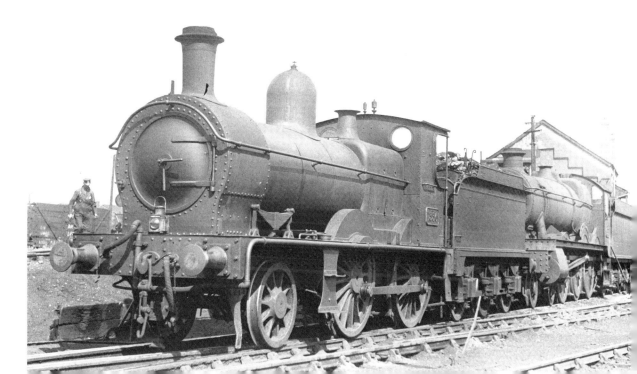

Above: Participants foregather at Broad Street station on 5 May, 1956, to inspect the motive power selected for the first stage of the LCGB's 'Poplar and Edgware' railtour, which was actually only the second in the long series of special trains organised by this club. Former North London Railway Class 2F 0-6-0T No 58859 was due to depart at 2pm for Poplar Dock on a tour extending over London Transport as well as both Eastern and London Midland Region territory. Designed by J. C. Park and introduced in 1879, there were originally 30 of these little goods tanks built at Bow up to 1905, and several were still working from Devons Road shed at this time. The Bluebell Railway purchased the last survivor, No 58850, which has reverted to its LNWR No 2650 carried from 1909-26.

Below: The last decade of steam brought increasing numbers of rail tour specials. Many of these were run to mark the closure of some hapless line, whilst others commemorated the passing of a particular class of locomotive, and often a combination of both. This was the LCGB's 'The South Western Limited' run on 18 September 1960. It started from Cannon Street and made its way back to Waterloo via Ascot, Fawley, Ringwood and Templecombe. Six different engines were employed, and the second stage from Ascot to Eastleigh was in the hands of former Wainwright SECR Class L 4-4-0 No 31768, of the series built by Beyer Peacock in 1914. It is making a photographic stop at Ropley, familiar today as the present outer terminus of the Mid-Hants Railway.

Above: On the grey, murky day of Sunday 26 November 1950, the Eastern Region mounted a special farewell journey non-stop from Kings Cross to Doncaster for the last Ivatt Atlantic to remain in service. Among the passengers was H. G. Ivatt, Chief Mechanical Engineer of the London Midland Region and son of the famous Locomotive Superintendent of the GNR. A large throng crowds around the grand old engine to pay their last respects shortly after arrival at Doncaster. LNER Class C1 4-4-2 No 62822 had been built there in 1905 as GNR No 294, one of 93 large-boilered Atlantics that so capably handled the principal expresses on the GN main line for 20 years prior to the advent of Gresley Pacifics. The prototype, No 251 of 1902, is preserved in the National Railway Museum.

Below: Early in 1957 the famous Dean GWR 'City' class 4-4-0 No 3717 City of Truro was taken out of the old Railway Museum at York, where it had been kept following withdrawal in 1931. It was repainted with its former No 3440 restored, returned to limited ordinary service and used for special publicity trains and railtours. In this view it was heading the RCTS' 'Moonraker' special from Paddington to Swindon Works past Iver on 18 August 1957. Built at Swindon in 1903, this engine was credited with having attained a speed of 102.3mph on the descent of Wellington bank with an up Ocean Mail express from Plymouth on 9 May, 1904. In 1963 it was again withdrawn, and this time placed in the GWR Museum at Swindon, thus achieving what many believe was the original purpose of this late enterprise.

Above: The last steam locomotive to be built for British Railways, Class 9F 2-10-0 No 92220 Evening Star, stops at Princes Risborough on 3 April 1960, whilst hauling 'The Six Counties Limited' special train from Paddington over the first stage to Yarnton via Maidenhead, High Wycombe and Oxford. Since it had only been completed at Swindon on 18 March that year, the LCGB had certainly wasted no time in securing its participation on their railtour, which was in fact its first passenger run. Introduced in 1954, the 251 engines of this magnificent class, incorporating the most advanced features of steam locomotive design, were doomed to obsolescence before they had hardly begun. All were restricted to a shamefully brief working life, and Evening Star was withdrawn from ordinary service as early as 1965. It obviously had to be preserved, and from its base in the National Railway Museum still operates on special services from time to time.

112